A HISTORIOGRAPHICAL STUDY OF LIVY
Books VI-X

A HISTORIOGRAPHICAL STUDY OF LIVY
Books VI-X

James Lipovsky

ARNO PRESS

A New York Times Company

New York • 1981

Editorial Supervision: Steve Bedney

First publication in book form 1981 by Arno Press Inc.
Copyright © 1978, 1981 by James Lipovsky
Reproduced by permission of James Lipovsky

MONOGRAPHS IN CLASSICAL STUDIES
ISBN for complete set: 0-405-14025-8
See last pages of this volume for titles.

Manufactured in the United States of America

Library of Congress Cataloging in Publication Data

Lipovsky, James.
    A historiographical study of Livy, books, VI-X.

    (Monographs in classical studies)
    Revision of thesis (Ph.D.)--Princeton, 1978.
    Bibliography: p.
    1. Livy. Historiae Romanae decades. Book 6-10.
2. Rome--History. I. Title. II. Series.
PA6459.L5 1981   937'.0072024   80-2657
ISBN 0-405-14043-6   AACR2

A HISTORIOGRAPHICAL STUDY OF LIVY:

BOOKS VI-X

by

James P. Lipovsky

TABLE OF CONTENTS

For Kathy

PREFACE

This work grew out of a dissertation which I submitted in 1978 to Princeton University. I wish therefore to thank once more Professor J. A. Hanson for his generous help at that time. To Professor T. J. Luce, who also read the dissertation, I owe a particular debt of gratitude. I have reaped continuing benefit both from his deep and sympathetic understanding of Livy and from his kind readiness to discuss the problems of the author. I wish also to thank Professor Ward W. Briggs, who read the entire manuscript and offered many useful suggestions. I am grateful to Steven Bedney of Arno Press for his kindness and patience in all our dealings. To Professor W. R. Connor I owe a conspicuous debt for his detailed criticisms and suggestions to improve this work. None of these men, of course, is responsible for any errors that remain.

With particular pleasure I acknowledge the joy and comfort I have found in my children, Elaine and Jimmy, during these times. Above all I am grateful to my wife, Kathy, for her patience and encouragement at all times and for her tireless assistance as a typist.

Columbia, South Carolina   December, 1980

FREQUENT SOURCES AND ABBREVIATIONS

In quoting Livy I have used the Oxford text throughout. I have indicated Livy's book numbers by Roman numerals, omitting these only when the book under discussion is obvious.

Abbreviations for works frequently cited are listed below:

Burck, Erzählungskunst	E. Burck, Die Erzählungskunst des T. Livius. Berlin 1934. Reprinted with a new introduction, Berlin/Zurich 1964.
Luce, Livy	T. J. Luce, Livy, The Composition of his History. Princeton 1977.
Ogilvie, Comm.	R. M. Ogilvie, A Commentary on Livy, Books 1-5. Oxford 1965.
Walsh, Livy	P. G. Walsh, Livy, His Historical Aims and Methods. Cambridge 1961.
Weissenborn	W. Weissenborn and H. J. Müller, T. Livi Ab Urbe Condita Libri. Berlin 1860-1864.

INTRODUCTION

If there has been a single judgment which, above all,
sums up the verdict upon the Ab Urbe Condita, it is this:
that the work is a "prose epic," its author a "poet in
prose."[1] The verdict is rather a slight than a compliment,
for praise of the work's "poetic" aspects has always been
overshadowed by blame of its shortcomings as history.

This attitude towards Livy has grown from a particular
set of beliefs about the way he composed his history.
Decades of scholarship in the nineteenth and early twentieth
centuries produced a damning picture of his working methods.[2]
Livy slavishly followed the accounts of his sources, often
even reproducing their judgments and their distortions of
fact. He did not think carefully about the actions which he
was narrating; therefore he several times related the same
event as if it were two different events (the so-called
"doublets"). He used only one source for each event, and did
not bother to read ahead to see in what direction his narrative was headed. Livy's personal contribution is therefore
evident mostly in his small-scale effects: style, the
construction of individual scenes and episodes, the moralizing

---

[1]This judgment is highly visible too: it appears on the
back cover of the Penguin translation of Books I-V.

[2]See the discussion in Walsh, Livy 138-172; Luce, Livy
xv-xxvii.

portrait here of a man, there of a family or nation. His
judgments are perceptible mostly in distortions of fact to
satisfy his patriotic urges or moral preconceptions.

The notion of a Livy who was almost completely enthralled
by his sources has created two great charges against him.
The first of these is that he has failed to impose a satisfactory large-scale organization or structure on the material
of his history. Ronald Syme says that he shows little skill
in grouping and interrelating events and "no instinct for
historical structure." P. G. Walsh speaks of "his inability
to impose upon the historical material an organized design, a
sense of control, and an acutely personal vision such as
Polybius and Tacitus manifest.[1] His history is widely viewed
merely as a long cavalcade of exciting and instructive scenes,
vivid illustrations perhaps of virtue and vice but with no
relationship to each other save their common moral concern.[2]
The second charge follows from the first. His preoccupation
with exciting and morally edifying scenes precluded a deeper
understanding of historical causation.[3] His history was at
its most profound when it recreated, in its most powerful
scenes, the authentic spirit of the past. Of historical de-

---

[1]Syme, Tacitus (Oxford 1958) 148; Walsh, Livy ix.

[2]Kurt Witte, RhM 65 (1910) 418-419 states this belief
most fully.

[3]Walsh, Livy 164: "Hence his narrative is more concerned with the attributes of the persons involved...than
with the significance of the changes themselves. Such emphasis on the personality of participants leads to a short-
sighted view of the issues."

velopment and its causes, however, he had no concept.[1] And
since he never held political office, he never understood
the processes by which decisions were made.

For all of these reasons Livy's fame traditionally
rests upon his reputation as a literary figure. As a historian, his reputation has been negligible.[2]

Against these notions of Livy has stood the work of two
scholars primarily, Erich Burck and T. J. Luce. Though Burck
in particular toiled for many years without significantly al-
tering scholarly opinion, the effects of his ground-breaking
work are beginning to be widely felt today. As long ago as
1934, Burck published Die Erzählunskunst des T. Livius in
which he challenged the view that Livy's history was merely
a string of episodes strung together. He showed that Livy,
by controlling the points at which books began and ended,
created a series of highly effective books, and an overall
sense of order, in the first pentad.[3] In 1950 he issued
a second study, Einführung in die dritte Dekade des Livius.
As in his earlier study on Books I-V, Burck found an overall

---

[1] R. G. Collingwood, The Idea of History (Oxford 1946) 44.

[2] Syme, The Roman Revolution 485-486 argues that Pollio's
criticism of Patavinitas (Quintilian I.5.56; VIII.1.3) attacks Livy's "moral and romantic view of history." He concludes, "Pollio knew what history was. It was not like Livy."

[3] R. M. Ogilvie has extended Burck's findings by developing the idea that individual books, if they do not have
full-fledged unifying themes, at least have an individual
"flavor" drawn from events therein: libertas in II, modestia
and moderatio in III and IV, pietas in V. Book I states the
greatness of Rome and intimates the themes of the other
books. Comm. 30-31, 233, 390, 526-527, 626.

structural control in XXI-XXX: the beginnings and ends of
books often coincided with important episodes. He also found
something more artistic: that the narrative of the whole
decade has a dramatic quality which makes the third decade
exciting to read. In 1977 T. J. Luce published Livy, The
Composition of his History, applying to Books XXI-XLV methods
similar to Burck's. He has found that Livy again ordered
his narrative so that major events were placed in emphatic
positions at the start, center, or end of his books.

The observations of these two men on Books I-V and
XXI-XLV implied that Livy was acutely aware of the sweep of
events in Roman history, that he identified the important
ones and placed them in emphatic positions within the structure of his work. How could such a picture be reconciled
with the plodding copyist, unaware of what lay in the future,
whom source critics portrayed? Luce's book tackled the problem fully. He demonstrated convincingly that Livy engaged in
a first stage of composition, preliminary to his actual
writing, where he read extensively among his sources, evalua-
ted the importance of various events, and "blocked out" his
material into overall units and groups. At this time he
reserved (when possible) the emphatic structural positions for
key episodes which were to get detailed treatment. His work
has thus made it possible--in spite of real blemishes in the
Ab Urbe Condita, like doublets--to ascribe to Livy himself the
responsibility for large-scale ordering of events.

There are those who would argue that an ancient historian

should be studied only for the light he sheds on ancient
history, and that his history should be praised or condemned
exclusively on the basis of its "accuracy:" that is, how
closely its conclusions approximate the conclusions of modern
scholarship. Livy, of course, could not and did not possess
the techniques by which modern scholars seek to unearth the
facts of ancient history.[1] To judge his results by the yard-
stick of our own knowledge is to apply a false test, one that
is unsympathetic to the problems Livy faced and the standards
of his day.[2] All too often, however, it is precisely this
test that has been applied. Livy's reputation has suffered
in two ways from this procedure. First, since accident has
preserved the early, not the late, portion of his work, we
have precisely those books where he was least able to solve
the problems which, as he was acutely aware, plagued the
early history. Second, such a procedure diverts attention
from an equally important question: what ideas or interpretations did Livy himself have about this period?

The purpose of this study is exclusively historiographical. I will in the first place examine the literary techniques which Livy employs in his narrative, and will stress
his ideas and interpretations on the period 389-293 which he
covers in his second pentad. An understanding of how accur-
ately and conscientiously he worked is more elusive, since
his sources for Books VI-X are almost completely lost. What

---

[1]Luce, _Livy_ xxv, 139-184.

[2]See Luce's remarks, _Livy_ xxv-xxvi.

we do know derives mostly from Livy's own discussions about
variant traditions in his historical authorities. Nevertheless, I will when possible compare his account to the other
accounts which were available to him. The conclusions to be
drawn from such a procedure are somewhat speculative and certainly tenuous; but they at least are more valuable than the
easy condemnations that he did not, single-handedly, unravel
the difficulties of Rome's early history.

In broad terms, then, this work will attempt to evaluate
the literary and historical achievement of Livy's second pentad. Even after the studies of Burck and Luce there is much
in Livy that is only imperfectly understood. Burck himself
seemed to regard the dramatic character of XXI-XXX simply as
a literary device. Luce wrote that Livy was no great master
of structure. He conceded too that Livy had relatively little
to say about history: "The traditional view...that Livy's
chief contribution to his history was in the adaptation of
individual scenes and episodes is probably true."[1]

It will be one aim of this study to argue that Livy seeks
to lend a dramatic quality not just to individual episodes in
Books VI-X, but to the overall narrative of the whole pentad.
The ongoing dramatic pace or "tempo" of the account gives the
whole pentad a well-focused ongoing literary effect. The
second aim follows naturally from the first: to demonstrate
that Livy was acutely aware of the "kinetic" in history, the
ongoing processes of development which mark the history of a

---

[1]Luce, _Livy_ xxvi.

nation.[1] It will be argued in these pages that the internal
dramatic tempo or movement of Books VI-X underlines important
historical developments. In advocating that ongoing developments are important in Livy, it is specifically not my intention to deny the importance of the moral themes which have
so occupied Livian scholarship. I insist, however, that they
are only a part of Livy's view of early history; they have
been erroneously taken to be the whole of it. Likewise, the
dramatic approach to the pentad is intended not to exclude
but to supplement and complete the structural approach set
forth by Burck and Luce. Indeed, important elements in the
structural design are frequently the key events in Livy's
dramatic and developmental interpretation. I believe this
study goes far beyond previous assessments of the Ab Urbe
Condita in several ways. It will illustrate a structure even
more carefully conceived that the structure of XXI-XXX, with
direct correspondence of several scenes to each other. It
will demonstrate that the whole account underscores real historical judgments about the ongoing developments of Roman
history. Avove all it will show the process by which the
literary method underscores these judgments, and will discuss
Livy's wider attitude towards the history of Rome. I shall
deliberately avoid speaking of Livy as a literary artist here,
a historian there; rather, he is a historian whose method of
exposition is dramatic.

---

[1]Only Luce, Livy 230-297 has perceived in Livy an interest in historical developments. He sees, scattered in various
passages in Books XXXIV-XLV, an exposition and explanation of
the incipient decline of the Roman character.

There is even reason to believe that this dramatic
exposition is part of the lactea ubertas which the ancients
(Quintilian X.1.32) found characteristic of Livy. Quintilian
used the term to contrast Livy's "milky richness" with the
brevity of Sallust; he was therefore referring immediately to
Livy's diction, rhythms, and elaborate periodic style.
Cicero's famous letter to the historian Lucceius (ad Fam. V.
12), however, seemingly applies the concept of ubertas to a
dramatic quality of writing. In the letter he urges
Lucceius to set aside a monographic section within his larger
history to cover events from Cicero's consulship down to his
return from exile.[1] The proposed starting and ending points
are particularly significant, for they make it easy to imagine
that Cicero envisioned unifying the account around the dramatic shift of his own personal fortunes. First would come
his vigilant defense of Rome in his consulship; then a difficult and trying time as his foes sent him into exile; and
finally the trump card, the justification of him and his
policies, his recall to the city. It is even easy to imagine
the final scene as Cicero might have planned it--a triumphant
return to Rome, throngs lining the Appian Way to cheer him as
the monograph comes to a dramatic (and self-congratulatory)
close. It is this dramatic process which he equates with
ubertas (V.12.2): "...if you will concentrate all your powers
on a single plot and character, I see in my mind's eye how

---

[1]V.12.4: "A principio enim coniurationis usque ad
reditum nostrum uidetur mihi modicum quoddam corpus confici
posse...".

much richer (uberiora) and more ornate everything will be."[1]
He is referring to a dramatic method exactly like that which
we will find in Livy, and it may well be that this dramatic
quality is an integral part of the milky richness of Livy.[2]

Many scholars have shown that Greek historians in the
Hellenistic period sought dramatic effects in their writing.[3]
The techniques of rhetoric and tragedy were particularly in
evidence. Episodes such as sieges or public debates were
dramatically constructed to evoke emotions like pity, fear,
or surprise. It seems, however, that dramatic structure and
emotional effect were always applied to the careers of individuals or to single historical episodes in Books I-V--a
practice which he continued into and beyond his second pentad.
The dramatic pattern which we shall see in VI-X, however,
where the dramatic narrative emphasizes and defines the ongoing process of historical change, represents an important
extension of the old techniques. In emphasizing historical
developments through drama Livy brought the dramatic technique

---

[1]"...si uno in argumento unaque in persona mens tua tota
uersabitur, cerno iam animo, quanto omnia uberiora atque
ornatiora futura sint."

[2]Surely it is apposite to note that Cicero sees these
dramatic vicissitudes as the most pleasurable aspect of
historiography (V.12.4): "Nihil est enim aptius ad delecta-
tionem lectoris quam temporum uarietates fortunaeque
uicissitudines." He explicitly compares the desirable features of his proposed monograph to the effects of dramatic
writing (V.12.6): "...secernas hanc quasi fabulam rerum
euentorumque nostrorum. Habet enim uarios actus mutationes-
que et consiliorum et temporum."

[3]For example, B. L. Ullman, TAPhA 73 (1942) 25-53; Walsh,
Livy 20-45.

to a new level; he surpassed both the work of the Hellenistic
historicans and his own work in the first pentad.[1]

Livy was faced--as any historian is--by two problems in
approaching a large body of evidence. First he needed to
indicate to the reader his interpretive thesis about the
overall trends in a period, and the significance of events.
Second, he had to acknowledge that certain events contradicted the general trends. Where Rome's power was growing,
she still suffered defeats. Relations between the social
classes, or orders, may have improved, yet there would be
examples of stress and strain anyway. How, then, was he to
show the proper perspective on events? A modern historian,
writing in the best scholarly journal, would openly state to
his reader the main direction of events. The second problem
he would solve by selecting important incidents in illustration of his thesis. Other events he would relegate to the
background, perhaps with a judicious acknowledgment that

---

[1]Burck, Erzählungskunst 181 finds no dramatic development beneath the narrative of I-V: "Das peripatetisch-
hellenistische Auswahlprinzip, mit dem letztere arbeiteten,
gibt es für ihn nicht. Davon vollends, dass Livius seine
Darstellung nach einem τέλος-Begriff im aristotelischen
Sinne orientiert hätte, wie es Polybios tat, Dionys versuchte
und von den römischen Dichtern Vergil sogar in kühner
Neudeutung der aristotelischen Formulierung wagte, kann keine
Rede sein." Contrast his views on the third decade, which he
believes to have a "vital quality" and a "dramatic tension."
He says, "This careful psychagogy impresses upon the structure
and course of the whole decade something of the style and
effect of a drama, as the hellenistic-peripatetic style demanded of a good work of history." Livy, ed. T. A. Dorey
(London and Toronto 1971) 25-26. My views on the literary
form of these books will appear in "Livy," forthcoming in
Ancient Writers: Greece and Rome, ed. T. J. Luce (New York).

certain incidents contradict the general trend. To Livy,
whose method of exposition is dramatic, not direct, such a
path is not open. And yet his solution, I think, resembles
that of our modern scholar. He solves the second problem by
playing down those events which he deems relatively unimportant. Conversely he elevates the important ones to a
larger status; we shall examine the means by which he does
this below. This process of deciding which incidents to
emphasize and which to de-emphasize has been widely regarded
as a deception, or the concealment of embarrassing facts. It
should be regarded instead as an indication of Livy's interpretation. He points out the main line of historical development, acknowledging events which do not conform to the
trends.

How does Livy solve the problem of imposing an interpretive thesis on events? The parallel of modern dramatic
historiography may be instructive. Barbara Tuchman's The
Guns of August, for example, adopts the thesis that the
Germans in 1914 can win the war only if they capture Paris in
their first offensive. This thesis dictates her interpretation of subsequent events: plans are seen as foolish or wise,
and battles as successful or unsuccessful, accordingly as
they affect the Germans' timetable for conquest. On a
dramatic level, her thesis causes the reader to see events as
a race against time. The Germans' attempt to attack in
Alsace, their decision to turn their axis of advance away
from Paris, and even the Russian advance on Tannenberg (which

causes a transfer of German troops from the West) all have
tremendous dramatic impact because they have been connected
to her initial thesis. Similarly, in accounts of the
Germans' 1941 invasion of Russia, it is a common thesis,
justified by Clausewitz, that the Germans can win only by
capturing Moscow before the onset of winter. Again, both the
historical significance and the dramatic impact of events
follow from this overall thesis. The decision to delay the
assault on Moscow in favor of one on Kiev, the first snowfall,
and the final desperate thrust at the capital in an early
winter, again are judged--and dramatized--in the light of the
overriding belief that the capture of Moscow would be
decisive. Dramatic historiography has given the Nazi
detachment, who see the spires of the Kremlin, a place in
modern history comparable to that of Hannibal after Cannae.
Both are symbols of ambition frustrated within an ace of its
goal.

Livy's method, though not identical to those above, is
quite similar. He makes certain scenes--speeches are
especially important in this connection--look forward and
declare that a particular issue will be especially important
in the future. The issue may be resolved later on by a
similar scene which, looking back through time, indicates that
the events of many years have been resolved in a particular
way. Speeches again are important in this function; so are
symbolic scenes where the course of a whole historical trend
is perceived in the deeds of an individual. The scenes which

both set and resolve the problems, as well as the important
events in between, are the very ones which receive dramatic
treatment as noted above. The cumulative effect of these
scenes, dramatic in themselves, is to create a carefully
worked dramatic pattern through the entire pentad which
traces the ongoing development of historical trends. Livy's
technique, then, is to allow events to seem to speak for
themselves; he delivers few judgments in his own person.[1]
And yet the presentation of the deeds has been carefully
molded and formed; from that process a larger historical
interpretation emerges with clarity.

The particular methods by which Livy emphasized
important scenes deserve to be set forth briefly. Partly
these methods are formal or direct, but mostly they are
dramatic. At a formal level, he generally devotes more space
to important incidents than to unimportant ones. Similar is
his practice of placing major incidents at the beginning,
center, or end of a book.[2] The placement of episodes can
even have a dramatic effect of its own; Livy is especially
fond of climaxing dramatic trends with important scenes at
the end of books. Their position there lends a note of
finality and resolution to the trends. Among strictly
dramatic techniques we may note the use of foreshadowing and
vivid language, like forceful direct discourse, to emphasize

---

[1]These judgments are generally moralistic: praise for
ancient virtue, and blame of recent vice.

[2]Luce, Livy 33-36.

major scenes. When treating an episode dramatically, Livy
seeks to heighten and increase his effects as the episode
progresses. The narrative of a battle, for example, may be
related in terms of increasing peril and desperation; in a
debate or quarrel, the emotions of the disputants may grow
ever hotter. Once the peak of danger or emotion has been
reached--that ·is, once the dramatic situation has been
exploited fully--Livy usually records the outcome of the
episode in just two or three sentences.[1] The increasing
emotion of a debate may be shown by a switch from indirect to
direct discourse or by such techniques as elaborate periodic
sentences, vivid series of questions, even the cadence of
the sentences themselves. Episodic structure is a particularly important device by which Livy shows rising tension in
a historical incident. This technique involves breaking
the narrative into segments, separating these segments by
internal "dividers" such as digressions or silent pauses, and
showing that tension rises as the narrative proceeds to each
new segment.[2]

It will be my aim, in the first two chapters, to trace
through Books VI-X the two historical trends which Livy saw
as important in this era: the struggle of the orders in

---

[1]K. Witte, RhM 65 (1910) 270-305, 359-419 analyzes
Livy's narrative techniques superbly.

[2]I do not wish to suggest that all episodes are important
which show some of these techniques. Certain episodes are
elaborated for other reasons: their popular fame, their usefulness as moral examples, or simply because they make good
reading. But it is correct to say that all important episodes
are distinguished by some--or many--of these devices.

Chapter One, and Rome's military expansion in Chapter Two.
I will record the episodes which pertain to these developments
and will show in the first instance how he makes the important
incidents stand out, while minor episodes or those which
actually contradict the main progress of events are treated
in a way that indicates their unimportance. Beyond that, I
will consider precisely what significance Livy assigns to his
important episodes and how he draws them together into a
larger dramatic pattern which underscores trends of great
historical importance. Having considered the individual
episodes and their overall effect, I will consider some wider
issues in the final chapter. Among these issues will be
Livy's attitude towards the historicity of events in VI-X;
whether he believed in "turning points"--that is, whether he
regarded historical change as slow or sudden; and what causes
he saw underlying historical change.

An interpretation such as this may still cause dissenting
rumbles from those who see Livy as a plodding copyist. Two
objections therefore deserve to be refuted at the outset.
First, it should not be claimed that he was indebted to his
sources for his overall viewpoint, as he of course was for
matters of factual detail. This view cannot be refuted
directly since the source tradition for Books VI-X has almost
wholly perished.[1] We may, however, cite against this

---

[1]Mostly this tradition is represented by fragments of
Dionysius of Halicarnassus, Livy's contemporary. He was not
Livy's source directly, but is generally thought to have used
the same traditions which were available to Livy. See Burck,
Erzählungskunst 5-6.

objection a general proposition: that historical interpretation is least likely to be derived from a source when it is
found where we find it in Livy: embedded in the overall
pattern and structure of the narrative. We may add evidence
of a more specific sort. A comparison of Books VI-X with the
corresponding fragments of Dionysius of Halicarnassus (and
others) suggests that Livy was responsible for key elements
in his historical interpretation. A military sedition in the
year 342 was seen by Livy as one of the central events in the
struggle of the orders; Dionysius apparently did not assign
it any such importance. Again when the practice of nexum, or
enslavement for debt, was abolished, Livy stressed the
importance of this action to the plebeians' freedom;
Dionysius did not. The harsh command of the consul Manlius
Torquatus, who executes his son for violating orders, assumes
a moral and historical importance--it exemplifies the antique
severitas--which it apparently did not have in Dionysius.
Livy turns a quarrel between the dictator Papirius and Fabius,
his magister equitum, into a moral counterpoint to the dread
imperium Manlianum, suggesting that proper military discipline
should be mingled with kindliness. While Dionysius' account
of this quarrel does not survive, not one of the many versions
which survive elsewhere interprets this incident as Livy did,
or assigns it as much importance. Dionysius emphasizes the
importance of granting Roman citizenship to Tusculum; Livy
does not comment on the issue until Rome extends her
citizenship widely after the Latin Rebellion. Then he draws

fully the philosophical implications behind extending citizenship and is best able to show the benefits which Rome's generosity conferred in the upcoming Samnite Wars.[1]

Nor, on the other hand, should it be claimed that Livy's historical interpretation was unavoidably imposed on him by the nature of events. His very divergence from Dionysius' interpretation reminds us that there is no single "right" interpretation imposed by events. This reminder is strengthened by even a cursory inspection of Livy's ideas. The provisions of the Licinio-Sextian Laws provide plebeians access to the consulship, agrarian reform, and the relief of debtors. Livy, however, focuses almost exclusively on the consulship and the issue at the philosophical heart of that controversy: are plebeians fit to hold the highest offices? Nothing inherent in the military conspiracy of 342 forced Livy to regard it (as he did) as a milestone along the path to civic harmony. He could easily have believed Rome's great bid for Italian hegemony began with the First Samnite War; instead he believed it began with the Second Samnite War. Besides, many of Livy's most important judgments are delivered in the form of speeches which may transcend immediate issues to review a broad spectrum of events. Decius Mus' speech on the Ogulnian Law, for example, reviews the performance of plebeians as curule magistrates for over fifty years. There is no evidence, then, that the major points of Livy's

---

[1]The episodes are treated below: military sedition, 64-65; end of nexum, 68-69; Manlius' harshness, 113-114; quarrel of Papirius and Fabius, 128 n.1; Tusculan citizenship, 104-105.

historical interpretation were copied out of his sources;
certainly they were not imposed by events themselves. The
historical interpretation should be assigned to this
historian--a statement which would be neither bold nor
surprising if Livy had received the sympathy and understanding
which he deserves.

How was it possible for Livy to create the dramatic
effects and structural design of which I have spoken? The
answer, as Luce has shown,[1] must be that he systematically
planned his structure: he drew up the major historical
events to be covered in a pentad and then allocated them
among the various individual books. In Books VI-X the
process went somewhat as follows. He saw that the struggle
of the orders at home and wars of expansion in Italy dominated the period. The major turning point in the foreign
wars--the point where local foes were finally crushed and
the greater wars for Italian hegemony were about to begin--
could be placed in the center of the pentad. Therefore the
outbreak of the Second Samnite War in 327 would begin the
second half of Book VIII; the defeat of the Latin Rebellion
and the rebellion's aftermath would end the first half of
Book VIII. This division places sixty-two years in the
pentad's first half, only thirty-five in the second half: a
strong indication that the division results from planning,
not chance.[2] Other major events, between which he perceived

---

[1]Livy 185-229.

[2]The discrepancy is reduced slightly if we allow for the

a thematic or historical link, he tried to balance symmetrically within his schema. The first major example in these
books of domestic strife, the sedition of Manlius in 385-384,
was placed at the center of Book VI. The last great example
of domestic strife, the quarrel of Decius and Fabius in 295,
was set at the middle of Book X, exactly balancing it. The
debate on the Licinio-Sextian Laws of 367 was put at the end
of Book VI. To balance this scene, a corresponding scene--
Decius Mus' speech on the Ogulnian Law in 300--came near the
start of Book X. Two other scenes, Manlius' execution of his
son and the quarrel of Papirius and Fabius, dealt with the
important moral issue of the ancient severitas. The former
was placed near the start of Book VIII; the latter, towards
the end. Within this basic framework it was still possible
for him to use book divisions advantageously; he sometimes
chose his beginnings and endings to unify books around important historical or thematic points, while in other books he
placed major scenes at the end to achieve dramatic emphasis.
The military sedition of 342 was chosen to receive emphasis
by its placement at the end of Book VII. In Book VIII a
special problem presented itself. That book spent much time
exploring the growing strength of Rome; but the humiliation
of Caudium in 321 lurked in the near future. Livy was able
to maintain the unity of effect in Book VIII by ending it
with Cornelius' victory over the Samnites in 322 B.C. The

---

fact that almost nothing is recorded in the five-year solitudo
magistratuum of 375-371 (VI.35.10-36.2).

Caudine defeat thus began IX; its effects would be nullified
through the course of the book--a process that culminates
with Rome's victorious conclusion of the Second Samnite War
at the end of IX. The Battle of Sentinum in 295, since it is
inseparably linked to the quarrel of Decius and Fabius, already fell neatly in the middle of X. Finally, Book X
covered much of the Third Samnite War; Livy desired to finish
X (and the whole second pentad) on a note of triumph. But to
carry the history as far as the defeat of Fabius Gurges in
292 would ruin the planned effect. Livy accordingly placed
the defeat at the outset of XI: the same method he had adopted
at the division between Books VIII and IX. He was thereby
enabled to end Book X, and the whole second pentad which had
seen so much expansion, with the defeat of the Samnites'
Linen Legion in 293.

This basic procedure of determining structure--balancing
certain incidents against each other, and placing other major
scenes to achieve suitable effects--requires the rest of the
material to be squeezed in between the important episodes.
Hasty treatment could sometimes result;[1] Book VII provides a
good example. Since VI ends with the Licinio-Sextian Laws of
367, VII must begin in 366. Yet Livy wanted to treat the
events of 343 and 342 (the First Samnite War and the military
sedition) at some length at the book's end: these two years

---

[1] Livy rejected what we might consider the obvious course
of simply lengthening a book that contained much material of
this sort. Though his books vary greatly in length from pentad to pentad, he keeps all the books within any one pentad
to about the same size. Luce, Livy 28-29.

receive fourteen chapters in all. As a result, fully twenty-
three years (366-344) must be treated in only twenty-eight
chapters. Livy uses the same technique in VIII where, in
order to link closely the grants of citizenship to the Latins
(in 338) and to Privernum (in 329), he compresses the intervening eight years into only five chapters (VIII.15-19).

These techniques--related episodes balanced symmetrically,
major scenes placed emphatically at the opening, middle, and
end of books, and the fitting (sometimes with great com-
pression) of the remaining material into the remaining
space--are identical to those which Livy employed elsewhere.
They clearly indicate that he not only reviewed the whole era
before writing and was himself responsible for the structure
of his history, but that he had given considerable thought to
the overall historical issues of the period and the relation-
ships between particular historical events as they affected
the development of these issues.

Many scholars believe that Books VI-X are not a self-
contained pentad, that they are strictly subordinate to a
decade, Books VI-XV, covering the conquest of Italy.[1] Particularly important, in this view, is the fact that the Third
Samnite War is still continuing at the end of Book X. Ronald
Syme sums up the opinion and the approach: "But the end of
Book X seems devoid of any significance. The historical

---

[1]R. Syme, HSPh 64 (1959) 30; E. Burck in Vom Menschenbild
in der römischen Literatur, ed. E. Lefèvre (Heidelberg 1966)
323-324; G. Wille, Der Aufbau des Livianischen Geschichtswerks
(Amsterdam 1973) 54-56.

break surely came a little later, in 290, with the two triumphs of M'. Curius."[1]

The genuine attraction of this argument lies in the fact
that the topics of peninsular rule and domestic peace cannot
be absolutely complete by the close of X. It is Book XI
which contains the end of the Samnite War and the plebeians'
succession to the Janiculum. We may speculate that Livy
created another bond between the second and third pentads:
a close correspondence of their central books, VIII and XIII.
We shall see that the sources of Rome's military might are
set forth in VIII.[2] While it is impossible to discover
whether Book XIII develops this topic cohesively, we may note
that it contained four very famous[3] _exempla_ of Roman morality; all the Romans killed in the first battle with Pyrrhus
were discovered to be facing the enemy; the Romans refused to
ransom their prisoners; Appius Claudius delivered a speech
urging rejection of peace terms with the victorious Pyrrhus;
and the consul Gaius Fabricius not only rejected a deserter's
offer to poison Pyrrhus, but sent him back to the king with
the story of his guilt. As Rome's military strength in the
second pentad finds its clearest expression in Book VIII, so
perhaps VIII and XIII together epitomize the military virtue
of the whole decade.

---

[1] HSPh 64 (1959) 30.

[2] See below, 101-140.

[3] The numerous sources which treat these incidents are
listed in T. R. S. Broughton, The Magistrates of the Roman
Republic, Vol. I (New York 1951) 190-194.

It is this writer's belief that the intricate structural
balance of Books VI-X indicates that Livy considered it a
self-contained unit. His use of drama by which he develops
major historical issues to satisfactory (if not final) conclusions points in the same direction. The judgment most in
accord with our evidence, then would be that Books VI-XV form
a decade, but one strongly divided into separate pentads.[1]
The method, however, which scholars employ to divide up
these books--and all the lost books--deserves further comment.
These divisions depend upon two elements: the Periochae, or
summaries of Livy's books, and the opinions of modern historians about where to locate historical breaks.[2] The procedure is full of pitfalls, for the Periochae, while generally
reliable in showing what events are covered in what books,
give no hint of Livy's particular interpretation and emphasis.[3]

---

[1]This is the view of P. Stadter, Historia 21 (1972) 294.
His findings are accepted by Walsh, Livy, Greece & Rome. New
Surveys in the Classics. No. 8 (Oxford 1974) 8, n. 3; and by
Luce, Livy 6.

[2]See the discussion in Luce, Livy 3-24, especially 10-14.

[3]The Periochae can in fact be every bit as misleading as
they are helpful. If the first decade were not extant,
scholars might well have divided up the first fifteen books as
follows. Book I would be a self-contained unit on the regal
period, followed by a decade (II-XI) on the struggle of the
orders. The decade would be divided neatly into two pentads
(II-VI, VII-XI) with major historical milestones at every
"break". Book II would begin with the foundation of the Republic causing the struggle of the orders to begin; the sum-
mary of II confirms the secession to the Sacred Mount among
other disturbances. The passage of the Licinio-Sextian Laws
at the end of VI would close the pentad with a major plebeian
victory. The whole decade would reach its natural culmination
with the final victory of the Hortensian Law at the end of XI.
Books XII-XV would follow as a tetrad on the wars with Pyrrhus.
All of these divisions could be surmised on the authority of

In no case do Periochae VI-X hint at the specific importance
which Livy saw in major episodes. Second, while Livy is
likely to recognize historical landmarks at the obvious
junctures where modern scholars specify them, it does not
necessarily follow that he will divide his pentads there. He
could choose a different "break"--one which might be dictated
(as it is at the end of X) as much by dramatic considerations
as by its inherent importance.

If Livy had chosen to continue VI-X beyond 293, he might
well have extended his account to 287, not 290. By so doing
he would not only be able to carry his military narrative
through the end of the Samnite Wars; he would also be able
to carry the domestic events through to the Hortensian Law.
And in fact Livy did use 287 as a divider--but at the end of
Book XI, not X.

Why did Livy end VI-X at 293 when the later date of 287
so readily suggested itself? There is a prosaic answer: he
may have simply concluded that there was too little material
available in his sources to support a full pentad on the
events of 286-265, a period of only twenty-two years. He
covered ninety-seven years in the second pentad (389-293),
forty-six in the fourth. Second, as he plotted out his overall structure, he surely saw how the division at 293 would
let him achieve the effects of balance and symmetry which we
have observed in VI-X, along with an excellent dramatic

---

the Periochae. But we do possess Books I-X, which show that
the above scheme does not correspond to Livy's actual plan.

resolution of the historical trends. Most significantly,
however, the decision to break at 293 avoids a full pentad on
the Pyrrhic War: an important decision which tells much about
his concept of the proportion and focus of the early pentads.
As it is, both the Samnite and Pyrrhic Wars are treated as
parts of a larger process: the conquest of Italy. Only with
the First Punic War in XVI-XX does Livy find a single war of
such importance that it merits a separate pentad. Even more
important is the Second Punic War, which is treated in ten
books (XXI-XXX). It would seem to destroy this proportion of
events if Livy divided Books X and XI in 287. Books XI-XV
would then become a separate unit devoted to the war against
Pyrrhus: a decision which would place the Pyrrhic War on an
equal rank with the First Punic War structurally. The new
proportion would not be indefensible. But it seems that
Livy's decision to end X in 293 indicates that he preferred
to subordinate the peninsular wars to the ones with Carthage.

Books VI-X have been largely ignored by scholars, who
have preferred to assess the later books against Livy's extant sources. And yet, as our earlier discussion indicates,
they offer a particularly rewarding look at Livy's historiography: the relationship of literary technique to genuine
historical judgment. The epoch itself assumed a great importance to him too.[1] It is within this century that he finds

---

[1]Livy considered these years important enough to treat
them (it would seem) at greater length than any of his
sources did. His account of the period before the Gallic
sack, by contrast, was much shorter than some. Luce, Livy
173-178.

Rome making its first great strides towards empire. Here
too was important progress towards reconciling patricians
with plebeians. At IX.16.19 he makes a remark unparalleled in
his history: this era exceeded all others in abundance of
virtues. I will contend that he saw these virtues not only
in the great individual exempla--and he lists several of
them at IX.17.7-11--but in the virtues learned by the whole
nation which allowed Rome to expand militarily while easing
her domestic crisis.

During our examination of Books VI-X we shall from time
to time have occasion to discuss some general literary techniques which have escaped scholarly attention. We shall
look closely at certain problems, peculiar to Livy, which
have gone unrecognized. Characterization in particular seems
to resist standard types of analysis; the characters who
people Livy's narrative often serve quite different purposes
than simply to embody good and bad morals.[1] Likewise, it is
demonstrably true that Livy depends on the reader's accepting
an obvious interpretation of a scene, even if reflective
examination yields quite different results. For example, in
Book VI Camillus advises his colleague Lucius Furius Medullinus not to join battle with the Volsci. The latter does engage them, however; he is on the verge of being defeated when
Camillus suddenly intervenes, winning the day for the Romans
and bathing himself in glory. A subtle interpretation might

---

[1]Walsh, Livy 82-109 gives a good discussion of many of
Livy's aims and methods in characterization.

perhaps be ventured: that Medullinus was in fact the protagonist of the scene. His decision to engage immediately was
in fact correct; once the Romans committed their full force
to battle, they won. It is Camillus whose strategic judgment
was wrong. Yet such an interpretation is forlorn. There can
be no doubt that Livy regarded Camillus as correct in the
dispute: he says so explicitly, and goes to great lengths to
glorify him; he even portrays Medullinus as admitting he was
wrong.[1] The resulting interpretation which I offer of Livy
may appear idiosyncratic in certain particulars, but I would
maintain that it is no more idiosyncratic than Livy himself.

The study of Livy has traveled, as Ogilvie has noted,
at a high level.[2] There is perhaps no better response to
Quintilian's charge (II.5.19) that Livy is for boys, and
Sallust for men, than to point to the distinguished line of
men--scholars, authors, and statesmen alike--who have been
drawn to him. It is as if a noble gens were turned out in
procession. In the train are modern scholars whose work has
done so much to advance the understanding of Livy: McDonald
and Walsh, Ogilvie and Luce, Witte and Burck. Held aloft
are the imagines of their predecessors, no less distinguished:
Madvig, Macchiavelli, Milton, Macaulay. If the present
study goes in any way beyond the achievements of these men,
it is intended to supplement, not replace, their work.
Indeed, I shall have no greater hope than for my efforts

---

[1]See the discussion below, 92-94, 130 n.1.

[2]Comm. vii.

to win the approval of those upon whose labors it has been built.

CHAPTER ONE

THE STRUGGLE OF THE ORDERS

INTRODUCTION

Before the second pentad begins in 389, the struggle of
the orders has already had a long and destructive history.
Throughout the first pentad Livy shows that the effects of
this struggle are inimical to liberty. Private individuals,
fired by immoderate ambition, seek to attain kingly power by
appealing to factionalism. Even more dangerous are the
external threats which develop because of the domestic
strife which has weakened Rome's military power. That these
dangers never overwhelm the state may be attributed partly
to the fact that Romans generally unite against extraordinary
dangers: for example, Spurius Cassius (II.41.8-10) or the
attack of Veii (II.43.4).

The outbreak of the struggle is traceable to the
expulsion of the kings, but its roots go back to the very
foundation of Rome. At that time the city is peopled by a
motley and undisciplined rabble: a point which Livy greatly
emphasizes.[1] The rule of the kings at least gives Romans a
chance to coalesce into a single people, united by ties of
soil and family; the state therefore does not fall apart

---

[1]Luce, Livy 246 n. 32 cites the evidence for Livy's
attitude. On early Romans see Luce, Livy 234-249.

when they are expelled (II.1.4-6). On the other hand the
people, who now control their own government, have not
learned to subordinate their own interests to a common good;
in Books II-IV Livy repeatedly stresses their inability to
work together. For this reason he attributes the struggle of
the orders to the expulsion of the kings, whose power alone
once repressed the struggle.[1]

The struggle of the orders has several other, more
immediate causes: the plebeians' desire for political offices, land, freedom from the crushing burden of debt, and
the patricians' determination to deny these things. Since
discord results from human vices, it can be remedied by
human virtues which will lead to acceptable solutions for
problems. These virtues are, as Ogilvie has pointed out,
moderatio on the part of patricians, and modestia for
plebeians. The patricians must show restraint in governing,
while the plebeians must show a corresponding restraint in
obeying lawful authority.[2] It is the ongoing mastery of
these social virtues which in Livy's view will therefore
represent progress towards political maturity.

A second idea which emerges involves the merits of the
plebeians. Are they capable of discharging the duties of
state? Or are they unfit to share responsibility? This

----

[1]II.1.4. Livy's belief that fear of authority was the
"glue" of early Rome's social and political fabric is shown
by the fact that he attributes the beginnings of actual class
strife to the death of Tarquin at Cumae (II.21.5-6).

[2]Ogilvie, Comm. 30, 390, 526-527.

issue is an important one, for, as the tribune Canuleius
says, the aid of all talented men is crucial if Rome is to
prosper (IV.3.13). It emerges most forcefully at IV.1-6
where the patricians vigorously deny the worth of the
plebeians.[1] Canuleius, perceiving the patricians' contempt
for his order,[2] asserts the positive abilities of the plebs.
With patricians and plebeians at loggerheads over the issue,
it is apparent (IV.1-4) that certain changes in the historical roles of the orders are necessary if Rome is to enjoy
the fullest help of her citizens. Recognition of the
plebeians' merit will therefore have two good effects: it
will help to end the struggle of the orders and will ensure
Rome's future prosperity.

Certain passages hint that plebeians will, in the future,
assume a greater share in the political process. Election of
plebeians to the quaestorship is seen as a step towards ultimately attaining the consulship (IV.54.6). When the
tribunate is restored after the expulsion of the decemvirs,
Valerius and Horatius speak of a future time when plebeians
will wield great power (III.53.10). Further, the plebeians'
struggle for power is regarded as an ongoing process, closely
linked with their enjoyment of liberty (III.54.9).[3]

Neither of these critical processes--the achievement of

---

[1]See, for example, IV.2.5-6.

[2]See, for example, IV.3.2-3, 3.7-8, 4.5-7.

[3]See also IV.5.5 on the connection between liberty and
a share of power.

harmony or the recognition of plebeian worth--has been carried through to its conclusion by the end of the first
pentad.[1] The first five books end, however, on a note of
hope and of challenge. A proposal is made at the end of V,
following the Gallic sack, that Romans should move to Veii.
Although the proposal is the work of the plebeian tribunes
(50.8, 53.3), Livy does not treat it as an internal dispute.
His mind has risen to a higher theme: the great dignity that
is Rome's. In a dramatically powerful touch, the people's
decision to stay and rebuild is said to ensure the city's
future greatness (54.7):

> Hic Capitolium est, ubi quondam capite humano
> inuento responsum est eo loco caput rerum
> summamque imperii fore; hic cum augurato
> liberaretur Capitolium, Iuuentas Terminusque
> maximo gaudio patrum uestrorum moueri se non
> passi; hic Vestae ignes, hic ancilia caelo
> demissa, hic omnes propitii manentibus uobis
> di.

It is a fitting conclusion to the first pentad, and excel-
lently paves the way for the realization of Rome's greatness,
beginning in Books VI-X.

These ongoing processes--the learning of _modestia_ and
moderatio, and the demonstration of the plebeians' merit--are
carried forward in Books VI-X, where they are at the heart of
the dramatic and historical development of the narrative.
Well-defined phases of the domestic struggle are treated in
the various books. The struggle is fiercest in Books VI-VII;
at the end of Book VII a reconciliation is effected. Strife

---

[1]The patricians continue to consider the plebeians unworthy of office: IV.54.7; V.14.4.

then fades into the background in Books VIII and IX, where
military events predominate: wars with the Latins and Samnites. Finally, in Book X the domestic struggle is revived
and brought to a satisfactory resolution.

BOOK VI

In Book VI the struggle of the orders, after a compara-
tive lull in Book V, revives strongly with the sedition of
Manlius Capitolinus. Scattered small scenes then indicate
that the struggle continues in the middle of the book.
Finally, the struggle over the Licinio-Sextian Laws shows
discord rising in a dramatic crescendo at the end of the
book.

Livy sees the sedition of Marcus Manlius (11.1-10,
14.1-20.16) as a major incident which renews the conflict
between the orders.[1] His account of the sedition details
the grievances of plebeians against patricians and uses
dramatic techniques to portray vividly Rome's domestic
strife.[2]

Livy states the plebeians' chief grievances clearly:
widespread debt, plus fear of enslavement for failure to pay

---

[1]There has been no great domestic strife since IV.59.10-
60.2. In Book V the siege of Veii and the fall of Rome push
domestic themes into the background. The struggle of the orders barely appears in the early chapters of VI (5.1-5, 6.1;
cf. 21.4.

[2]To indicate the importance of the sedition he devotes
over nine pages in the Teubner text to it; a major scene.
The Teubner text is useful for comparing the relative lengths
of scenes because its pages contain no critical apparatus and
therefore maintain a reasonable standard length.

--a fear on which Manlius capitalizes (11.8-9). By relating
vividly the single case of a centurion--here the symbol of
the plebeians' honorable service and ill-merited sufferings[1]
--he most forcefully illustrates their grievances against
patricians (14.3-8). Livy stresses the centurion's courageous service in Rome's foreign wars (14.3, 14.6). His
courage in battle and his labor to rebuild at home, however,
have drawn a poor reward from the patricians: he has con-
tracted massive debts, and been reduced to poverty by
remorseless usury (14.7).[2] Now, having defaulted on his
debts, he is being haled into bondage (14.3-5).[3]

It is an easy matter in this situation to portray
Manlius' hold on the plebeians' loyalty. When he intervenes
to save the centurion (14.3-5), the gratitude of the latter
is vividly presented. He hails Manlius as "his liberator,
the father of the Roman plebs" (14.5: liberatori suo, parenti
plebis Romanae; cf. 14.7-8). Although this one act has already bound the plebeians to him, Manlius inflames them to

---

[1]The fact that the centurion remains nameless increases
his universality. Livy's sympathetic treatment of the centurion indicates that he regards the plebeians' petitions for
relief as justified, even though he naturally disapproves of
Manlius' conspiracy.

[2]The money-lenders are of course patricians; see 14.3.

[3]Cf. the old soldier at II.23.2-7. Livy uses a very
similar technique at X.34.4-14. There, instead of relating
individually the capture of several abandoned towns, he
dramatically recounts at length the capture of only one (34.4-
13), then briefly notes the capture of the others (34.14).
There, as here, Livy captures vividly a whole series of
events in one specific case.

follow him per omne fas ac nefas by selling his estate for
the benefit of debtors (14.9-10). His demagogic claim that
the patricians have hidden the Gallic ransom sets the tone
of strife for the events which follow (14.11-13).[1]

To achieve dramatic impact Livy has thereafter divided
the narrative into episodes and has shown that tension rises
with each one[2]--until, in a sudden twist (18.16-20.16),
Manlius is condemned to die by a vote of his own plebeian
supporters. The whole account--which is to be regarded as a
dramatic unity, the Arisotelian ὅλη καὶ τελεία πρᾶξις[3]--
therefore emphasizes the ill feelings between the orders.

The next scene (15.1-16.4), a confrontation between
Manlius and the dictator Aulus Cornelius Cossus, begins with
a short respite (15.1: Ita suspensis rebus) before the
sedition moves into its next phase: open struggle (15.2:
adesse certamen). The antagonism between the orders is
emphasized by military terminology (15.2-3) and by Manlius'
accusations that patricians are deliberately repressing the
plebeians with dictatorships and usury while cheating them
of the Gallic treasure (15.7-13). When Cornelius orders
Manlius jailed, the plebeians go into mourning.

At the start of the next scene (16.5-17.6) matters have

---

[1]That he is a demagogue has already been made clear at
11.3-8, 14.2.

[2]In the first scenes (11.1-10, 14.1-13) Livy has already
shown the "outbreak" (11.1: grauior domi seditio exorta) and
"spread" (14.1: gliscente in dies seditione) of the sedition.

[3]On Livy's use of this technique see Burck, Erzählungskunst 182 ff; Walsh, Livy 178-180.)

come near to outright sedition (16.6: <u>Iamque haud procul</u>
<u>seditione res erat</u>). This scene, which records the
plebeians' thoughts on the incarceration of Manlius, builds
its dramatic power on their growing emotions. Livy takes
pains to show the growth of the seditious spirit in
well-defined stages. After plebeians spurn the patricians'
attempt to placate them by sending a colony to Satricum, they
become more open in supporting Manlius (16.7-8: "...remedio
inritatur seditio. Et iam magis insignis et sordibus et
facie reorum turba Manliana erat...". Next, in several
sentences of indirect discourse, they are reminded of the
evils which patricians have worked on them and their cham-
pions; they must not abandon Manlius (17.1-5). The plebeians
become so incensed[1] that they now threaten to free Manlius
(17.6): "Iam ne nocte quidem turba ex eo loco dilabebatur
refracturosque carcerem minabantur...". Finally, Manlius'
release from jail, far from ending the tension, makes it
worse than ever (17.6): "...remisso quod erepturi erant ex
senatus consulto Manlius uinculis liberatur; quo facto non
seditio finita sed dux seditioni datus est."

The brief annalistic digression at 17.7-18.1, covering
embassies at the end of the year 385 and the new magistrates
for 384, is skillfully used to create an effective dramatic
pause.[2] This pause has two effects: it impressively empha-

---

[1]The use of anaphora (17.2) and rhetorical questions
(17.3-5) pointedly expresses their anger.

[2]The pause is a favorite Livian device; see, for example,
X.27.8-9 before the Battle of Sentinum. Closely related is

sizes the plebeians' wrath at 17.6, and makes the force of
the sedition to seem renewed at 18.2.

Tension finally comes to a head at 18.2-15. The absence of a foreign war allows each side to gird for the upcoming clash (18.2). Strife is clearly worse than before;
a showdown is at hand (18.3): "Igitur cum pars utraque acrior
aliquanto coorta esset, iam propinquum certamen aderat. Et
Manlius...consilia agitat, plenior aliquanto animorum ira-
rumque quam antea fuerat." Manlius' speech in oratio recta
(18.5-15)--deliberately more vivid than the oratio obliqua
of 17.1-5--climaxes the strife of the entire narrative. The
rift between the orders receives its usual emphasis: the
patricians are inimici (18.8, 18.9, 18.10); the domestic
struggle is a war (18.5-6). Especially dramatic is his
conclusio (18.13-15) which exhorts the plebeians to greater
assaults: they must impose a ruler on the patricians, destroy
the consulship and dictatorship, and end trials of debtors;
he will lead the way.

Just as the sedition has reached the highest pitch of
intensity, Livy records the patricians' successful attempt to
detach Manlius' plebeian support by accusing him of seeking
regnum (18.16-20.16). He finds two obvious difficulties in

the insertion of silences at critical moments; see E. Dutoit,
Mélanges J. Marouzeau (Paris 1948) 141-151. On a larger
scale, Livy interrupts his narrative of major events by
switching scenes for dramatic effect; for example, the sieges
of Saguntum (XXI.7.1-9.2, 11.3-12.3, 14.1-15.2) and Abydus
(XXXI.16.6-17.11, 18.5-9). See Walsh, Livy 196; Luce, Livy
55 n. 36; idem, TAPhA 102 (1971) 280-281.

Manlius' conviction and execution.[1] First, Manlius' ardent supporters in sedition turn against him (20.5). Second, no historian offers Livy any specific evidence for the charge of regnum (20.4).[2] Given these difficulties, it is interesting to note the historian's procedure. He affirms--what else could he do, given the fact that Manlius was executed?--that surely the evidence for the charge must have been solid (20.5). And to indicate the loss of plebeian support--which must have also occurred--he seems to add a sentence in which Manlius obliquely seeks the title of rex (18.15).[3] He states later that plebeians do in fact become convinced that Manlius threatens their liberty (19.4, 19.6-7, 20.5, 20.13-14).

The death of Manlius, however, does not bring an end to the discord. While the plebeians do order his execution, Livy points out that the duty is hateful to them (20.11). Moreover, the commoners quickly regret their action (20.15). Thus the episode ends without any rapprochement between the orders; discord breaks out anew as the narrative closes.

Scattered incidents maintain civil discord as a prominent issue during the middle scenes of Book VI. At

---

[1] Livy's sources do insist that Manlius was executed (20.5, 20.12).

[2] "Cum dies uenit, quae...pertinentia proprie ad regni crimen ab accusatoribus obiecta sint reo, apud neminem auctorem inuenio...". Cf. 18.16.

[3] "...uos si quo insigni magis imperii honorisue nomine uestrum appellabitis ducem, eo utemini potentiore ad obtinenda ea quae uoltis." This sentence would seem to be Livy's own invention since, if he had found it in his sources, it would have substantiated the charge of regnum.

27.3-28.4 the plebeians' demand for relief from debt by a
censorial review is not met (27.3-5). They angrily protest,
and claim that Rome's foreign wars are merely designed to
distract them from political action (27.6-7). They accordingly resolve to obstruct the military levy and the judgment
of citizens for debt pending the satisfaction of their
demands (27.8). When an attack by Praeneste requires military response, the plebeians persist in their purpose until
the enemy's arrival at the Colline Gate causes them to
relent (27.9-28.4). Livy's description of the ensuing battle (29.1-8) does not have a peripeteia; such is the Romans'
superiority that, once united, they simply sweep the enemy
from the field and rout him from all his fortresses in a
swift campaign. Livy thereby points up the lesson that
civil strife dangerously limits Rome's might.[1]

After a year of domestic calm (30.1-9), debt once more
causes the tribunes to block the levy during a military emer-
gency, until finally the senate agrees to a temporary
cessation of the war-tax and of the judgment of debtors
(31.1-5). No sooner, however, is the victory won than the
plebians, their political leverage gone, are forced to submit
once more to legal judgments for debt and an increased tax
(32.1-4). In their broken state, they do not even resist
conscription into three armies to fight the Latins and Volsci
(32.4-5).

---

[1]On the danger of internal discord, cf. 31.6, etc. On
the benefits of unity, cf. IV.60.1, etc.

The account of the Licinio-Sextian Laws (34.1-42.14)
has a double importance. First, it revives the thematic
question of the plebeians' ability to hold high office.[1]
This it does by focusing almost exclusively on the bill which
would give plebeians access to the consulship, rather than
the proposals on land and debt.[2] Second, it raises the
tempo of domestic strife to a dramatic climax at the end of
the book.

When the patricians oppose the opening of the consulship
to plebeians, the plebeians recognize that their very competence to hold curule office is in question (37.8): "...non
esse in plebeiis idoneos uiros ad curules magistratus."
They respond that this view has been discredited by events.
Plebeians have already served the government well both as
military tribunes and quaestors (37.8-9); if given the
chance to serve as consuls, they will acquit themselves
honorably (37.11).

Patricians, however, are unwilling to credit them with
such talents. In a very important speech Appius Claudius,
their spokesman,[3] denies that plebeians are competent to
hold the consulship (40.15-41.3). Furthermore, he insists
that the strictures of religion disqualify them from office
(41.4-10).

---

[1]See above, 30-32.

[2]The solution to problems of debt and land is seen as
ancillary to the opening of the consulship: 35.1, 37.1-2.

[3]The Claudii appear as the plebeians' special enemies in
the early books of Livy; II.27, 29-30, 56-61; III.44.54;
IV.6, X.7. See Walsh, Livy 89-90.

At 40.15-41.3 Claudius angrily equates the election of plebeians with the election of unqualified men (40.19): "'Timeo' inquit, 'ne, si duos licebit creari patricios, neminem creetis plebeium.' Quid est dicere aliud 'quia indignos uestra uoluntate creaturi non estis, necessitatem uobis creandi quos non uoltis imponam'?" The result of the bill, he says, will be the election of consuls on the basis of opportunism, not merit (41.1): "...occasionibus potius quam uirtute petere honores malunt."[1] Indeed, he sums up his first objection by referring to the plebeians' "unworthiness" (41.4: indignitate) to be consuls.[2]

To this objection he adds a second: the plebeians' religious status disqualifies them from the consulship. He is merely citing accepted practice when he reminds his audience that only patricians can hold the consular auspices (41.7).[3] But he pointedly emphasizes the patricians' superiority over the plebeians in this regard (41.6). The commoners' sharing in the auspices he haughtily condemns as

---

[1] Contrast with this the attitude of plebeians, who regard their merit as equal (35.2): "...conando agendoque iam eo gradum fecisse plebeios unde, si porro adnitantur, peruenire ad summa et patribus aequari tam honore quam uirtute possent."

[2] Throughout, his attitude towards the plebeians is scornful. He implies that they cannot judge what is best for themselves (40.5), chides them for not acting like free men (40.6-7, 40.12), and even challenges their ability to render fair judgments (40.14).

[3] The plebeians, however, would surely reject this estimate of their religious status, nor would they agree that they cannot hold the auspices; see IV.6.3.

pollution and sacrilege, a mockery of religion (41.8-9). In
short, Claudius does not merely state that plebeians cannot
hold the auspices. Instead, he emphasizes their inferiority
to the patricians and scorns them as unworthy to hold the
auspices.

The challenge to the plebeians, then, occurs at both
the human and divine level: are plebeian magistrates competent to discharge the duties of office, and are they acceptable to the gods? The same questions were raised at
IV.1-6. Then there was no means to resolve the issue since
the plebeians were barred from high office.[1] The passage of
the Licinio-Sextian Laws (42.9-11), however, will allow the
plebeians' worth to be judged, for the first time, by the way
they handle the supreme authority of the state. Livy's
account of the debate directs the reader's attention to the
important issues for the future. Will plebeians in office
prove their competence? Will they be acceptable to the gods?
And will they persuade the patricians of their worth?

Episodic structure is used here, as it was in the
Manlian sedition, to emphasize the powerful domestic strife
which attended the contest over the Licinio-Sextian Laws.
The account is divided into three sequences (34.1-35.10,
36.7-37.12, 38.3-41.12) and a denouement (42.9-14). Livy
dramatically shows the growth of discord within each individual sequence; and each successive sequence is carefully shown

---

[1]Surprisingly, even the later election of plebeians to
be military tribunes does not seem to bring up the issue of
competence forcefully: see V.12.8-13, 13.2-3, 18.1-6; VI.30.1-2.

to be more discordant than the last. Digressions, which
punctuate the dramatic narrative and heighten the effects of
growing tension, are inserted between all three sequences and
the denouement. The portrayal of increasing tension and
strife is therefore at the heart of Livy's narrative plan.

The first sequence (34.1-35.10) sets action in motion
towards the great struggle with the tale of Ambustus' slighted
daughter (34.5): "...parua, ut plerumque solet, rem ingentem
moliundi causa interuenit." At the outset are described the
plebeians' abject condition and political weakness (34.1-4).
Yet, spurred on by the burden of debt, they are soon girding
themselves for an upcoming struggle (35.1-2). The tribunes
Gaius Licinius and Cucius Sextius propose legislation on
land, debt, and the consulship; these sweeping measures will
cause great struggle (35.5): "...cuncta ingentia et quae sine
certamine maximo obtineri non possent." With the conflict
now underway, both sides resort to heavy-handed tactics to
gain their ends. Patricians gain the vetoes of other tribunes
to block the proposals (35.6-7). Sextius' threats to block
elections, given in oratio recta, bring the dramatic tension
to a climax (35.8-9). Livy quickly ends the sequence by
noting the state of the conflict: the two tribunes, continu-
ally returned to office, allow no curule magistrates to be
elected for five years (35.10).

After a digression on war with Velitrae (36.1-6), the
second sequence (36.7-37.12) shows an increase in the domestic
tension (36.7): "In maiore discrimine domi res uertebantur."
The increasing momentum of the plebeians' initiative is

suggested by three factors (36.7-8): Licinius and Sextius
have been reelected to their eighth tribuneship; they have
received the open support of Fabius Ambustus; and the number
of tribunes opposed to the laws has been reduced from eight
to five. The rest of this sequence is devoted to indirect
discourse in which Licinius and Sextius show the strife
between the orders and the need for their proposals to become
law. Only through their own consuls will plebeians end
oppression in the matters of debt and land (36.11-37.4).
Further, one consulship each year must be reserved by law
for a plebeian; otherwise the patricians will usurp both
consulships in spite of the plebeians' merits (37.4-11).
Their oration moves the plebs, but action must be deferred
until the army returns from the siege of Velitrae (37.12).

After a brief interruption to record the army's return
and the magistrates for a new year (38.1-2), the third
sequence (38.3-41.12) portrays the final struggle over the
laws (38.3): "Principio statim anni ad ultimam dimicationem
de legibus uentum...". The sequence features two speeches:
one representing the views of Licinius and Sextius, the
second by Appius Claudius. A brief introductory section
shows that both sides believe the decisive moment is approaching: emotions are at fever pitch as they prepare for a final
showdown. The patricians see it as their "final recourse"
(38.3: ultima auxilia) when they name Camillus dictator; the
tribunes respond by arming their followers with great courage
(38.4). Camillus is "filled with anger and threats" (38.5:

plenus irae minarumque) and "aroused with anger" (38.8:
percitus ira) as he forbids Licinius and Sextius to pass the
laws over their colleagues' vetoes. The tribunes are rather
inflamed than intimidated by his threats (38.9).

When Camillus' abdication leaves the bitter contest
still unresolved (38.9), it is the speech of Licinius and
Sextius (39.6-12) that provides the decisive push. This
speech, coming at a time when plebeians are becoming disenchanted with the law de plebeio consule (39.1-2), kindles
them for a final effort (39.5). The tribunes indicate that
a critical point has been reached. Their proposals are no
longer blocked by a dictator, foreign war, or dissenting
colleagues; it is now the plebeians who stand in the way of
their own interests (39.8). In a powerful conclusio
(39.11-12) the tribunes challenge the plebeians to decide
what they want. They will receive all three bills together,
or will have none at all. The tribunes' resolve to press
the legislation through seems to represent the renewed determination of the plebeians generally.[1]

---

[1]This speech usefully illustrates Livy's narrative
method. Its effect is to show irresistible pressure by the
united plebeians against the patricians' opposition, as
Claudius' hopelessness at 40.2 and Livy's direct statement at
39.5 ("...acerrime accenderent...plebem...") confirm. Livy
shows the plebeians' ongoing progress towards passing the
Licinio-Sextian Laws only partly by the straightforward
narration of events: the decreasing opposition of tribunes,
etc. Equally important are the frankly emotional effects:
the rising anger, even the vigorous cadence of the prose
sentences. Thus it is here in a speech, not in the revelation of any new facts, that the plebeians seem to make their
decisive push. We should note, however, that the speech is
delivered when the plebeians become suddenly disenchanted
with the proposal to have plebeian consuls (39.1-2). This

Against this determination, Appius Claudius can only
argue (40.3-41.12) in vain; the struggle is nearing its
end (40.2): "Ap. Claudius Crassus, nepos decemuiri, dicitur
odio magis iraque quam spe ad dissuadendum processisse...".[1]
The speech again emphasizes the internal discord: he despises
his opponents (40.2), and they hate him (40.3, 40.13). He
especially attacks Licinius and Sextius as ambitious and
dangerous (40.7-12). We have already noted his objections to
plebeian consuls on the grounds of incompetence (40.15-41.3)
and sacrilege (41.4-10). The scornful tone of Appius'
speech vividly indicates the strife between the orders.
Likewise his conclusio (41.11-12), which claims that the
bills would depopulate the countryside and destroy all human
society, shows how wide a chasm separates plebeians and
patricians. Even more importantly, Livy has created a
dramatic climax to the whole conflict over the Licinio-Sextian

---

failure of resolve is somewhat anomalous, as plebeians feel
no doubts about this bill either before (38.5) or after
(see 40.2, 42.9). Livy, it would seem, admits the anomaly
into the narrative in order to occasion the tribunes' speech.
This failure of resolve causes a further difficulty because
it forces the speech's conclusio to direct its challenge not
to patricians but to plebeians, that they should accept all
three bills. It seems, however, that on an emotional level,
if not a logical one, the conclusio increases tension against
patricians; that Livy intended this to be its authentic effect is shown by the plebeians' fire at 39.5 and Claudius'
hopelessness at 40.2. It is not rare for a scene to assume
a role in Livy's narrative which is justified by its emotional
effect, not by reflective analysis of its factual or logical
contents. See 26-27, 92-94, 129-130, 130 n.1.

[1]Cf. 42.1: "Oratio Appi ad id modo ualuit ut tempus
rogationum iubendarum proferretur."

Laws by following the oratio obliqua of 39.6-12 with oratio
recta here.[1]

The final dramatic pause (42.1-8) directly foreshadows
the imminent resolution of the conflict (42.1): "Oratio Appi
ad id modo ualuit ut tempus rogationum iubendarum proferretur."
Further, the creation of five plebeian decemuiri sacrorum
seems to clear the path to the consulship (42.2): "...gradu-
que eo iam uia facta ad consulatum uidebatur."

With the plebeians' victory thus foreshadowed, Livy
resolves the clash in a swift denouement (42.9-14). The
passage of the three laws receives less than one sentence
(42.9). It is notable that Livy places little emphasis on
the restoration of harmony: a clear indication that, while
the specific dispute has been resolved here, the more general
struggle of the orders abides. Indeed, harmony is usually
restored at the end of domestic conflicts, but generally
does not endure.[2] Though Rome does in fact celebrate the
restoration of harmony at this point (42.12-14), there is no
reason to expect it will last. The Licinio-Sextian Laws are

---

[1]Oratio recta is used elsewhere for climactic effect,
just prior to the final resolution of scenes: VII.40.4-19,
XXI.13.1-9, XXXI.18.2-4, etc. At VIII.34.11, after a long
speech in oratio obliqua, Livy quotes the final sentence to
achieve this climactic effect. Walsh, Livy 212 notes that
oratio recta achieves similar dramatic impact at the end of
dialogues: "Sometimes both parties in the dialogue use it
[sc. oratio recta], but more often it is reserved for the
final comment, thus adding emphasis to the explosive
indignation so frequently expressed."

[2]For example, the orders achieve concord at III.65.5-7,
but it is undone immediately. Cf. VI.20.15, etc.

forced on an unwilling patrician class (42.9).[1] Other
terrible disputes are also noted, which are only composed
when the plebs concede the new office of praetor to the
patricians (42.10-11). And indeed, it is clear almost immediately in Book VII that the struggle of the orders has come
no closer to resolution than before.[2]

The dramatic impact of the conflict over the Licinio-
Sextian Laws can hardly be overrated. It is important not
only for its vivid portrayal of domestic strife, but for its
emphatic position at the end of the book. Placed there, it
is the capstone of Book VI. The action of the book, dominated
by strife throughout, culminates in the vivid description of
the disorders associated with Licinius and Sextius. Book VI
thus emerges as a dramatic unit which shows the struggle of
the orders building to a climax. In spite of the resolution
of the immediate quarrel, relations between plebeians and
patricians remain tempestuous as the book ends.

BOOK VII

Book VII portrays the ongoing development both of the
struggle of the orders and of the debate on the plebeians'
merit. The defeat of Lucius Genucius in battle inflames the
patricians to assert anew that plebeians are unfit to be
consuls. When, amidst great strife, they begin to usurp

---

[1]"...per ingentia certamina dictator senatusque uictus,
ut rogationes tribuniciae acciperentur; et comitia consulum
aduersa nobilitate habita...".

[2]See below, 49-50.

both consular positions, the plebeians see that their competence has been challenged. A victory won by Popilius
Laenas soon demonstrates, to the plebeians' satisfaction at
least, that their talent cannot be questioned. More importantly, Marcus Valerius Corvus, a patrician of popular
sympathies, acknowledges their worth; he exhorts them to
follow the highest standards so that they might demonstrate
their merit to all. As in Book VI, the domestic struggle
culminates in an important final scene: a military conspiracy.
Here, however, Livy portrays a major reconciliation between
the orders, as both sides come together on the basis of
modestia and moderatio.

Two small quarrels occur near the beginning of Book VII.
At 1.4-6 the patricians, in the face of criticism, open the
curule aedileship to plebeians; at 3.9-4.3 Lucius Manlius
Imperiosus' harsh levying of troops causes the plebs to haul
him into court. In the first major scene (6.7-12), Livy
revives the question whether the plebeians ought to serve
as consuls. The case of Lucius Genucius, the first plebeian
to lead an army into battle, is seen as a test of their
qualifications (6.8): "In exspectatione ciuitas erat, quod
primus ille de plebe consul bellum suis auspiciis gesturus
esset, perinde ut eunisset res, ita communicatos honores pro
bene aut secus consulto habitura." When Genucius leads his
army into an ambush and loses his life in the subsequent rout

(6.9),[1] the patricians see it as proof of their contention
that plebeians are unfit for high office (6.10-11).[2] It is
important to note that the occasional blunders of patrician
commanders have no such general significance. At VI.30.2-6
two patricians completely mishandle a military campaign:
they send out foragers without reconnoitering, rashly believe
a story (planted by the enemy) that the foragers have been
surrounded, then fall into an ambush while hastening to their
aid. By their "rashness and stupidity" (30.6: _temeritate_
atque _inscitia_) they suffer even the loss of their camp. Yet
their defeat does not impugn the order as a whole; patricians
have too frequently proven their merits. Thus it must be
with plebeians. They stand, as it were, at the beginning of
a long road; they shall prove their worth only when they have
established a similar record of excellent service. Only thus
will they be able to refute accusations, based on individual
cases, that they are unfit for office.

The next ten chapters (7.1-17.6) represent a lull in
the struggle of the orders; they deal almost exclusively
with wars against various enemies: the Gauls, Hernici,

---

[1]Livy describes the defeat itself in one cursory sentence. The event's real significance is that it shows the
patricians' attitude towards plebeian consuls in general.

[2]"...irent crearent consules ex plebe, transferrent
auspicia quo nefas esset; potuisse patres plebi scito pelli
honoribus suis: num etiam in deos immortales inauspicatam
legem ualuisse? uindicasse ipsos suum numen, sua auspicia,
quae ut primum contacta sint ab eo a quo nec ius nec fas
fuerit, deletum cum duce exercitum documento fuisse ne deinde
turbato gentium iure comitia haberentur."

Tiburtes, Tarquinienses, Privernates, Veliterni, and
Falisci. The scattered cases of domestic strife are all
brief; they do not contribute to any dramatic effect. At
12.4, for example, Livy refers very simply to a sedition
nipped in the bud.[1] At 13.9 the plebeian army, clamoring
for battle, reminds its commander that they have been sent as
soldiers into battle, not as slaves into exile. A certain
amount of friction also arises over the reduction of interest rates (16.1) and over the evil precedent of Gnaeus
Manlius, who summons the Tribal Assembly in camp (16.7-8).
Taken as a whole, however, these chapters represent a dramatic
"trough" in the struggle of the orders. Tempo, however, requires variety of tension; great scenes are dramatic only
insofar as they stand out against a plainer background.[2]

At first glance, the narrative at 17.6-25.2 seems no
more elaborate than in the preceding sections. In some
seven and one-half chapters Livy covers about seven years.[3]
The account therefore is little more than a skeletal record

---

[1]Weissenborn, ad·loc. believes that a colorful anecdote
in Cicero (Brutus 14.56) probably refers to this sedition.
If so, it is entirely possible that Livy also knew the tradition, but omitted it in favor of an uninterrupted, albeit
brief, account of the defeat of the Tiburtes.

[2]This principle, so basic to Livy's narrative technique,
was apparently not apprehended by Dionysius, whose speeches
are called "interminable" by Walsh, Livy 230-231. For example, after the secession to the Mons Sacer Dionysius records
ten speeches covering thirty-eight chapters (VI.49-86); Livy
limits himself to a few lines of oratio obliqua (II.32.5-12).

[3]Events are included from the last half of 356 through
the initial notice of magistrates for 349.

of facts, where various events in the struggle of the orders
are interrupted, for example, by events abroad[1] and by the
lists of annual magistrates. In segments such as this, the
historian seems to have little scope to give special interpretation to points of importance. As a result many years
may pass by quickly, yet tediously.

In this case, however, Livy achieves remarkably cohesive
effects both of theme and tempo. By careful composition, he
focuses dramatic attention back on the struggle of the orders
and shows that the plebeians are beginning to demonstrate
their abilities in office. Several techniques are employed
to achieve these effects.

In attempting here to narrate the struggle of the orders
coherently, Livy is faced with a particular difficulty.
Certain events, such as the debtors' relief, tend to recon-
cile the plebeians to the State; others, such as the
patricians' usurpation of both consulships, tend to do the
opposite. Accordingly, even though most of the incidents
demonstrate strife,[2] there is a danger that 17.6-25.2 will
seem but an ill-digested hodgepodge of harmony and discord.
Livy overcomes the problem by dividing the period into
"phases"--first one of strife (17.6-21.4), then of concord
(21.5-22.7), finally again of strife (22.7-25.2). He

---

[1]See 17.8-9, 18.2, 19.1-4, 19.6-20.9, 21.9, 22.4-6, and
23.2-24.9. Sometimes, as at 17.8-9, these events are linked
to the struggle of the orders and the interruption minimized.

[2]See 17.7, 17.9, 17.10-18.1, 18.3-10, 21.1-4, 22.7-10,
22.10-23.1, and 24.10-25.2.

sharpens the effect by marking off each phase from the
others by an appropriate topical sentence. After the sometimes bitter divisions of part one, the restoration of
harmony is clearly announced (21.5): "Inclinatis semel in
concordiam animis noui consules fenebrem quoque rem, quae
distinere una animos uidebatur, leuare adgressi...". The
resumption of strife is likewise marked (22.7): "...professus
censuram se petere C. Marcius Rutulus, qui primus dictator
de plebe fuerat, concordiam ordinum turbauit...".

More strikingly, certain events receive special interpretation to fit in with the overall effect of each phase.
For example, the election of patricians to both consulships
causes no strife in phase two because plebeians are grateful
for their recent[1] relief from debt (22.2). Elsewhere, however, it is the very burden of debt which causes plebeians
to accept two patrician consuls.[2] In phases one and three
Livy emphasizes strife. In the first phase Livy stresses
the plebeians' abject financial state even as he mentions
that they have obtained relief from usury (19.5). In the
last, he states that Fabius Ambustus is appointed dictator
so that the Licinian Law will not be observed in the consular
election (22.10)--even though it was Ambustus' first cousin
who helped to pass the law. It is difficult to avoid the
impression that Livy has slightly "wrenched" the interpretation

---

[1] See 21.5-8.

[2] See 19.5-6. Weissenborn, ad VII.21.3 rightly cites
VI.32.3 as a parallel case.

of incidents in order to amalgamate them into a coherent
account.

During these same chapters Livy uses the "point-
counterpoint" method to show that the plebeians are proving
their merits; that is, the patricians challenge their competence at the start, but are refuted by the evidence of
Popilius Laenas' deeds at the end. The patricians' contempt
for the commoners is immediately apparent. They consider
the appointment of the first plebeian dictator beneath the
dignity of the office (17.7): "Id uero patribus indignum
uideri etiam dictaturam iam in promiscuo esse...". Furthermore, they succeed in regaining control of both consular
positions for the years 355, 354, 353, 351, 349, 345 and 343.[1]
Their determination to monopolize the office reflects their
scorn for the plebs (18.3-4). The plebeians are quick to see
the implications of this attitude: they are considered no
better than slaves (18.5-7).[2]

To refute the patricians' contempt, Livy recounts at
length the prowess of a plebeian consul, Marcus Popilius
Laenas, in battle (23.2-24.9). Popilius prepares for battle
with the thoroughness typical of Rome's finest commanders

---

[1]The impressive language of 17.13-18.1 indicates the
importance of the patricians' breakthrough.

[2]"Plebes contra fremit: quid se uiuere, quid in parte
ciuium censeri, si, quod duorum hominum uirtute, L. Sexti ac
C. Licini, partum sit, id obtinere uniuersi non possint? uel
reges uel decemuiros uel si quod tristius sit imperii nomen
patiendum esse potius quam ambos patricios consules uideant
nec in uicem pareatur atque imperetur sed pars altera in
aeterno imperio locata plebem nusquam alio natam quam ad
seruiendum putet." Cf. 18.9.

(23.5); he increases his tactical advantage by engaging the
Gallic enemy as they charge uphill, and routs them (23.8-10).
When the Gauls rally on level ground, Popilius is forced to
retire from the line briefly after receiving a wound while
inter primores (24.3). It is his return to the field which
provides the dramatic peripeteia to the engagement (24.4):
"Iamque omissa cunctando uictoria erat, cum consul uolnere
alligato reuectus ad prima signa "quid stas, miles?' inquit
...". Livy thus portrays Popilius as the central figure in
the successful battle. When two patrician consuls are
elected for 349 (24.10-11), the plebeians are able to point
out the obvious lesson: they have proven their merits in
high office (25.1): "Prius quam inirent noui consules mag-
istratum, triumphus a Popilio de Gallis actus magno fauore
plebis; mussantesque inter se rogitabant num quem plebeii
consulis paeniteret...".

The effectiveness of the plebeians' verdict at 25.1 is
greatly enhanced by the fact that it is presented as the
final and decisive judgment on merit in this section of the
history.[1] We should note two techniques by which Livy
achieves the well-defined structure of a patrician challenge
refuted by the excellence of plebeian deeds. First, he
records no disparaging comments later about the plebeians'
worth at 28.1 and 28.9-10, where the patricians regain both
consulships (during the years 345 and 343). By omitting any

---

[1]Thereafter the issue of merit is quickly submerged in
the incursions of Gauls and Greeks and the First Samnite War.

reference to merit there, Livy allows 25.1 to retain its
authority as the final statement. Second, Livy reserves all
his emphasis on plebeian excellence for the one example of
Popilius, which follows and refutes the patrician challenge.
He could easily have stressed earlier victories by plebeian
commanders. As early as 9.1, only one year after Genucius'
defeat, Gaius Sulpicius captured Ferentinum from the Hernici
in cooperation with his patrician colleague. Marcus Popilius Laenas himself won a victory, also in conjunction with
his patrician colleague, outside the very walls of Rome
(12.3-4). Plebeian consuls won victories on their own as
well: at 11.2 and 11.7-9, at 16.3-6, and at 17.1-2, where
again Popilius was the victorious commander. The first
plebeian dictator conducted a successful campaign at 17.6-9,
while at 15.9-10 not only did the plebeian consul win a
battle but his patrician colleague was defeated. Yet in
none of these contexts did Livy suggest that plebeians were
demonstrating their capacity for office. By treating their
abilities only at 23.2-25.1, Livy accomplishes two things.
First, simply in recording the events since Genucius' defeat,
he has built up a considerable record of plebeian success to
substantiate the favorable assessment of their skills at 25.1.
More importantly, this particular victory, coming after the
patricians' objections to plebeian consuls, adroitly refutes
their criticism. Livy is thus able to end the sequence by
"correcting" the patricians' judgment.

Another lull follows in the domestic struggle during the

next chapters;[1] domestic affairs then become submerged in
the opening of the First Samnite War.

The plebeians' merit is confirmed on one final occasion
in Book VII: an address by Marcus Valerius Corvus to his
troops in the year 343 (32.12-17). The election that year
of Valerius, himself a patrician, together with a patrician
colleague marks the last time when the Licinian Law is not
observed (28.10). Corvus' remarks underscore the plebeians'
great advance: no longer do patricians have an advantage in
gaining public office, as they once did. More importantly,
he equates the rejection of birth with the recognition of
merit (32.13-14):

> Fuit cum hoc dici poterat: patricius enim
> eras et a liberatoribus patriae ortus, et
> eodem anno familia ista consulatum quo urbs
> haec consulem habuit: nunc iam nobis patribus
> uobisque plebei promiscuus consulatus patet
> nec generis, ut ante, sed uirtutis est
> praemium.

Accordingly, he exhorts the plebs to seek for themselves the
course of highest honor (32.14). Valerius offers himself as
a model worthy of their emulation: he has won highest honors
not by schemes, but by deeds (32.12).[2] His advice sets for
the plebeians a standard by which, as they serve in office,

---

[1]The State appears harmonious at 26.12 and 27.1-4. Nor
does Livy record strife in cases where he might have done so:
28.3 (a harsh levy), 28.9 (legal judgments against usurers),
and 28.10 (the election of two patrician consuls).

[2]"'Facta mea, non dicta uos, milites' inquit, 'sequi
uolo, nec disciplinam modo sed exemplum etiam a me petere.
Non factionibus [modo] nec per coitiones usitatas nobilibus
sed hac dextra mihi tres consulatus summamque laudem
peperi.'"

they might demonstrate true merit.

Book VII, like Book VI, culminates in a major scene of domestic conflict. Here it is a military conspiracy in the year 342 (38.5-41.8) which Livy portrays as part of the struggle of the orders. In the resolution of this crisis, however, Livy stresses that the patricians finally adopt an attitude of moderatio; the plebeians respond in a spirit of modestia. Here at last, then, Livy believes Romans have mastered those civic virtues which are the heart of any enduring domestic peace.

The military conspiracy is clearly presented as a movement of plebeians against patricians. Its root cause is said to be poverty and debt (38.7).[1] Further, the conspirators' hatred and fear are fixed upon the patricians (39.4-5) --even though it is the plebeian consul, Gaius Marcius Rutulus, who forestalls the conspiracy.

In this episode Livy stresses with particular eloquence the evils of the domestic struggle. When the conspirators under Titus Quinctius are about to attack Rome itself, Marcus Valerius Corvus, who commands the defending army, delivers a speech emphasizing the unthinkable horrors of civil war (40.4-14). He vividly appeals for harmony, citing their common gods (40.4-5), the countryside (40.6), previous secessions (40.11), and the exemplum that even Coriolanus'

---

[1]Weissenborn, ad VII.39.10 rightly compares 41.1, where Titus Quinctius calls the conspirators miserorum ciuium. In other seditions Livy also, quite naturally, equates the army with the plebeians: cf. II.32, III.50-54, etc.

Volscian troops ceased fighting upon the entreaty of Roman
women (40.12).[1] Civil war is truly inconceivable (40.14):
"Postulate aequa et ferte; quamquam uel iniquis standum est
potius quam impias inter nos conseramus manus."[2]

Most important is Livy's remarkable use of the characters of Valerius and Quinctius to show that patricians and
plebeians have finally learned moderatio and modestia. This
discussion raises particularly interesting and important
problems about Livy's general technique of characterization--
problems which we shall first consider in detail before showing how these two men illustrate the important moral
learning which takes place here.

Even the most prominent characters in Livy's early books
create very little impression of individuality. By and large
they embody a particular point of view (for example, the
Claudii), perform a particular function (for example, the
kings) or represent a range of moral traits. Certainly
there is truth in the common view that Livy deliberately
portrays individuals as exempla of particular virtues.[3]
He himself urges his readers to imitate examples of good, and
to avoid the bad (Preface 9-10). And yet to claim that his

[1]See II.40.1-10 where, however, the decisive appeal was
addressed to Coriolanus himself, not the Volscian troops.

[2]See 40.9: "...uos--horreo dicere--hostes." See also
the vivid description of battle (40.10) and Valerius'
admonition that it is more honorable to flee than to do battle against one's country (40.13). Cf. Quinctius' patriotic
emotions at 40.16.

[3]See Walsh, Livy 82-109; Mary Ann S. Robbins, Heroes
and Men in Livy, Books I-X (Unpublished diss. Bryn Mawr 1968)
passim.

characters are moral _exempla_ is hardly to claim that they
have a complex literary or historical function. That is,
Livy must, by the very nature of his task, associate men
with deeds. It is but the shortest step, and no great literary achievement, to note that these deeds reflect moral
qualities.[1] To evaluate Livy's characters as moral _exempla_
is, admittedly, to lay bare an important element in his admiration of early Rome. This approach, however, obscures the
equally important problem of the dramatic function of characters: how do they advance the action of the narrative? The
treatment of Valerius indicates that he is primarily treated,
not as a three-dimensional character, nor yet as an _exemplum_
of virtues (which, admittedly, he is), but as a kind of
dramatic prop. He is strictly subordinate to the reconciliation of the orders at the end of Book VII. Towards this
end, he is drawn at some length in Book VII as a champion of
the plebeians (see below). Throughout the rest of his long
career, however, Valerius Corvus becomes as colorless as the
majority of Livy's heroes; far from drawing his character
further, Livy does not even maintain his image as a plebeian
champion. Nowhere is this more evident than at X.9.3-6,

----

[1] I am attracted by the example of news reporting. If an
article on the society page states that Mrs. John Doe gave a
garden party on behalf of the local hospital, surely that reveals something of Mrs. Doe's philanthropic character. It is
equally sure that this is not literary characterization.
Livy seems much like the reporter, save that he points out
the salutary moral lessons of the deeds which he reports. I
do not of course deny that subtler characterizing touches can be
found in Livy; but is their scarcity, not their commonness,
which provokes comment.

where Valerius carries a law of appeal. Even here, where the
context virtually demands some reference to his love of the
plebs, Valerius receives only a perfunctory notice as the
man who passed the bill.[1]

In Book VII, however, Valerius' plebeian sympathies are
very strongly portrayed.[2] Not only does he support their
admission to the consulship (32.12-16), but he has shared
their portion of battle (32.11). He explicitly professes his
concern for them at 32.15-16, where he plays on his cognomen
Publicola (=populum colere).[3] In sketching Valerius'
character at 33.1-3 Livy emphasizes his familiarity with the
people; it testifies to Valerius' popularity among the plebs
that his soldiers follow him "with incredible eagerness"
(33.4: incredibili alacritate) into battle.

These earlier references to Valerius' special relationship with the plebeians are now recalled as he faces Quinctius'
rebellious army. He is said to love all the citizens,
especially the soldiers (40.3).[4] It is critically important

---

[1] After Book VII Valerius reappears in the following
passages: VIII.3.5, 16.4-12, 17.5; IX.7.15, 17.8, 17.12,
40.11-13, 40.21, 41.1; X.9.3-6, 9.7, 11.3-6. The Valerius at
VIII.35.10-11 is probably Corvus' son, while Livy is probably
referring to Corvus himself at X.3.3-6, 4.3-5, 4.12-6.1,
9.3-6, 9.7. See T. R. S. Broughton, The Magistrates of the
Roman Republic. Vol. 1 (New York 1951) 148 n. 2 and 170 n. 2.

[2] On the plebeian sympathies of the Valerii see Walsh,
Livy 88-89.

[3] "Non, si mihi nouum hoc Coruini cognomen dis auctoribus
homines dedistis, Publicolarum uetustum familiae nostrae cognomen memoria excessit; semper ego plebem Romanam...colo atque
colui."

[4] "...Coruinus omnes caritate ciues, praecipue milites, et
ante alios suum exercitum complexus." The conspirators served
under Valerius the previous year (40.6).

to note that he uniquely embodies the quality of <u>moderatio</u>,
the exercise of self-control in a position of authority
(40.7-9):

> Ego sum M. Valerius Coruus, milites, cuius
> uos nobilitatem beneficiis erga uos non
> iniuriis sensistis, nullius superbae in uos
> legis, nullius crudelis senatus consulti
> auctor, in omnibus meis imperiis in me
> seuerior quam in uos....Quod meum factum
> dictumue consulis grauius quam tribuni
> audistis? Eodem tenore duo insequentes
> consulatus gessi, eodem haec imperiosa dic-
> tatura geretur; ut neque in hos meos et patriae
> meae milites ⟨sim⟩ mitior quam in uos--horreo
> dicere--hostes.

Valerius therefore inspires great confidence when he offers
the conspirators, as an alternative to dreadful civil war, a
fair settlement of their grievances (40.14): "Postulate aequa
et ferte...".

The emphasis on Valerius' character has been directed
towards establishing this point: that the selection of a
moderate man to compose the sedition represents a shift in
the policy of the whole patrician class towards moderation.
Quinctius points out this lesson explicitly (40.17-18):

> Qui pugnarent uobiscum infestius, et alios
> duces senatus habuit: qui maxime uobis, suis
> militibus, parceret, cui plurimum uos,
> imperatori uestro, crederetis, eum elegit.
> Pacem etiam qui uincere possunt uolunt: quid
> nos uelle oportet?

The characterization of Quinctius, the leader of the
conspirators, is if anything more striking. A man of peace
himself,[1] he urgently advises his men to accept reconcilia-

---

[1]T. Quinctius plenus lacrimarum ad suos uersus 'me
quoque' inquit, 'milites, si quis usus mei est, meliorem
pacis quam belli habetis ducem.'" See also 40.14.

tion: they should respond with trust to "known fidelity"
(40.19: cognitae...fidei). He therefore gives expression,
on the plebeian side, to the ideal of modestia. This portrayal of Quinctius' character creates a problem for Livy.
He engages on the one hand in sedition; and yet he must
command a certain moral authority if he is to be a convincing
exponent of modestia. Livy solves the problem in a way that
can only be called remarkable: he portrays Quinctius as
innocent of any crime. He is described as a man of no ambition (39.11): "...attulerunt T. Quinctium in Tusculano
agrum colere, urbis honorumque immemorem." The conspirators
doubt that he will help; so resolving on threats and force
(39.13) they drag him off to their camp (39.14). Even as
imperator Quinctius is "stunned" (39.15: exterrito); he is
disassociated from the march on Rome (39.16): "Suo magis
inde impetu quam consilio ducis conuolsis signis infesto
agmine ad lapidem octauum uiae, quae nunc Appia est,
perueniunt...". Livy says that he is worn out fighting even
for his country, let alone against it (40.3). Valerius
prefaces his remarks to Quinctius with remarkable prescience
of his unwillingness to rebel (40.13): "T. Quincti, quocumque
istic loco seu uolens seu inuitus constitisti...". There is
little wonder, in short, that Quinctius finally pleads inno-
cence as his defense in the conspiracy (41.2); he has had no
role as its leader, other than to help Valerius end it![1]

---

[1]Livy exculpates others when it suits his literary purpose: VIII.20.11, 32.15. See below, 108-109, 119, 123.

The portrayal of Valerius and Quinctius, then, is
dictated by Livy's desire to make then symbolize the larger
moral change--the adoption of _moderatio_ and _modestia_--which
he sees in the happy resolution of the conspiracy. At
41.1-2 the conspirators unanimously applaud Quinctius' proposal that they put themselves into Valerius' hands. Nor
are they disappointed, for their estimation of the patricians'
moderation is borne out by results. Valerius, with the
senate's approval, secures an amnesty for the conspirators
plus certain improvements in the soldiers' condition (41.3-4).
One provision, that no soldier's name might be stricken
from the rolls against his will during a campaign, protects
the goods of debtors from seizure while they are in the
service.[1] The other, that no military tribune should serve
afterwards as first centurion, provides a signal example of
harmony. Publius Salonius, against whom the law is directed,
secures its passage by beseeching the senate not to value his
honor more highly than the public concord (41.5-7).[2]

Livy, then, sees the military conspiracy as important
to the restoration of harmony; Book VII ends with the orders
reconciled. It is instructive to note the contrast with
Dionysius. His account of the conspiracy does not survive.

---

[1]B. O. Foster, _Livy_ (London and Cambridge 1967) Vol. 3,
510 n. 3.

[2]Other annalists listed further concessions, which
Livy neither accepts nor rejects (42.12): that usury was
forbidden; that no one might hold the same magistracy within
ten years, or two offices at once; and that both consuls
might be plebeians.

Yet unlike Livy, he apparently did not portray the sedition
as a closed matter, for he later says (XV.4.5) that Manlius
Imperiosus executed his son to put an end to disturbances
such as this one. Since the effects of the sedition endure
that long it would seem unlikely that he portrayed it as
resolved at this time by the restoration of domestic
concord.[1]

BOOKS VIII AND IX

The struggle of the orders is not prominent in Books
VIII and IX. Indeed, though these books do record a few
notable events in the struggle, Livy himself comments on the
absence of discord in this period (IX.33.3): "Permulti anni
iam erant cum inter patricios magistratus tribunosque nulla
certamina fuerant...". Incidents in the struggle are so
few that they create no dramatic effect. As a result, the
restoration of harmony at the end of Book VII seems to carry
over into a period of relative tranquillity, if not complete
domestic peace, in these books.[2]

Among the incidents where the struggle of the orders

------

[1]Perhaps thematic considerations even influenced Livy's
choice of sources. He cites a variant (42.3-6) according to
which Valerius never served as dictator; matters were handled
by the consuls instead. This version would presumably make
it more difficult to portray a great figure of moderatio
since Valerius, like all members of his gens, is particularly
friendly to the plebs. Perhaps even worse would be the fact
that the variant apparently did not emphasize concord at all.
Although the armies refused to fight, the commanders never
spoke of a reconciliation of the orders (42.5): "...nec ab
ducibus mentionem concordiae ortam...".

[2]The absence of domestic strife is largely the natural

flares up, the sharpest is the conflict in 339 (VIII.12.4-5, 12.8-17). In this year the patrician consul Tiberius Aemilius Mamercinus, angered by the senate's denial of a triumph, carries out his office "in the manner of seditious tribunes" (12.10: _seditiosis tribunatibus similem_). Thereafter, with both consuls opposing the senate, the affair becomes a regular struggle pitting the plebeians and consuls against the patricians (12.11). Hoping to limit the consuls' power, the senate bids Aemilius name a dictator against the Latins; he names his colleague, Quintus Publilius Philo (12.12-13). His dictatorship is popular because of its denunciations of the senate and its pro-plebeian, anti-aristocratic legislation (12.14). His laws provide, _inter alia_, that plebiscites are to bind all the citizens, and that one of the censors must be a plebeian (12.14-16).[1] Just as Livy introduced these events on a note of strife (12.4-5), so now he ends them with the nobles' gloomy verdict upon the year (12.17); the opening and closing sentences thus help to unify the account around the motif of strife.

At IX.26.8-22 an investigation against various conspiracies causes the old patrician _nobiles_ to turn their

---

result of the fact that Books VIII and IX deal primarily with military affairs: the Latin War and Second Samnite War. J. Briscoe in _Livy_, ed. T. A. Dorey (London and Toronto 1971) 18 n. 11 gives the following approximate ratios of domestic to military activity: only 30/70 in VIII and 26/74 in IX, compared with 57/43 in VI and 43/57 in VII.

[1]In emphasizing the struggle of the orders, Livy even interprets another law, which allows the senate prior approval of bills in the Centuriate Assembly (12.15), as a popular victory.

wrath against the plebeians. They claim that it is the "new
men" who ought to be investigated for conspiring; they
threaten the plebeian dictator, Gaius Maenius, and his
(patrician) master of the horse with legal action (26.11-12).
The patricians' hostility is in fact the prime force which
causes these two, as well as Publilius Philo, to be put on
trial. All three defendants, however, are gloriously ac-
quitted (26.20-21). Livy condemns factions here, and gives
in Maenius an example of proper conduct by a public figure
(26.13-22).

The patricians still occasionally register their dis-
pleasure with plebeian magistrates. A plebeian dictator
comitiorum causa is, with transparent bias, declared uitio
creatus by the patrician augurs (VIII.23.16).[1] Patricians
likewise oppose the appointment of the first plebeian praetor.
Their resistance, however, is halfhearted since the plebeians
already possess the highest magistracies (VIII.15.9). The
issue of the plebeians' merit has become quite unimportant
in these books, however. Their worth is not even mentioned
when laws are passed which require one censor to be plebeian and
recognize that plebiscites bind the whole people (VIII.12.15-
16). Nor does Livy mention that Quintus Publilius Philo, a
plebeian, was the first consul whose powers were prorogued
beyond his first year (VIII.23.12). We may at least note,
however, that Livy himself freely numbers plebeian magistrates

---

[1]"...cui non apparere, quod plebeius dictator sit, id
uitium auguribus uisum?"

on his list of great Romans (IX.17.8, 17.13) in recognition
of their contributions.

Livy recognizes debt as one of the three great problems
facing the plebs, along with the acquisition of land and
political offices. Accordingly he devotes a scene to the
abolition of nexum, where he shows the worst abuse of the
debtor eliminated (VIII.28.1-9). History has associated the
demise of this institution with the cruelty of a single man,
Lucius Papirius. Livy therefore recounts Papirius' crimes
against Gaius Publilius in detail: he tries first to seduce
the youth; spurned, he resorts to threats; finally, he has
Publilius scourged (28.2-5). Interestingly, there is no
hint that this matter pits patricians against plebeians;
indeed, quite the opposite is true. The people, taking
pity on the lad, receive the help of the senate, which bids
the consuls to introduce a law abolishing nexum (28.6-10).
Tension between the orders here is rather eased than intensi-
fied.

A comparison of Livy's account with the version extant
in Dionysius of Halicarnassus (Roman Antiquities XVI.5)
reveals a great deal of similarity. Although Dionysius dates
the event after the Caudine Forks, both agree that the youth[1]
was handsome; that he was bound over in payment of a paternal
debt; that he resisted his master's importunities; that he
was whipped for his resistance and fled into the Forum,

---

[1]Dionysius, however, gives the lad's name as Publius
rather than Publilius.

stirring popular wrath; and that his suffering ended the
practice of nexum. Yet they differ significantly in point
of view. Dionysius relates the events as the private story
of Publilius; hence he identifies his father as a military
tribune who went under the yoke at Caudium, specifies that
Publilius' debt was to bury his father, and states that
Papirius[1] was sentenced to death for his crime. That this
incident ended nexum is added only as an afterthought.

Livy, by contrast, emphasizes the larger significance
of the incident to the plebeians (28.1): "Eo anno plebi
Romanae uelut aliud initium libertatis factum est quod necti
desierunt...". Accordingly he does not identify Publilius'
father, and merely refers to the debt as aes alienum paternum
(28.2). Like Dionysius, Livy sympathetically recounts
Publilius' sufferings; yet Livy does not even mention that
Papirius was brought to trial, much less sentenced. Instead,
he is concerned to present the chain of events by which
Publilius' case ended nexum. The crowd's anger results not
in a trial but in senatorial action: the consuls are directed
to introduce a law that only a debtor's goods, not his person,
might be liable for debt. Thus Livy portrays, if not a
lessening of debt, at least the lighter punishment of debtors.

In the final scene of Book IX Livy clearly indicates
that a new phase in the domestic struggle will be coming
(46.1-15). The admission of plebeians to high office has

---

[1]Dionysius does not give Papirius' name; this detail is
found in Livy.

made their role in public affairs less controversial. At
the same time, from their sharing of high offices a new
privileged class has begun to emerge: the patricio-plebeian
nobility. The domestic struggles of the late Republic will
be waged along these new lines: the urban mob versus the
patricio-plebeian nobility. Neither is the old struggle
between patricians and plebeians over at this point, nor is
the new phase by any means well underway.[1] We do have here,
however, the first indication of a shift away from a struggle
of patricians and plebeians to a conflict between nobles and
the urban mob.

The man who plants the seed of this new discord is
Gnaeus Flavius,[2] a freedman's son. Elected curule aedile,
under controversial circumstances according to some versions
(46.2), he fights inflexibly against the nobles, who despise
his low birth (46.4). He pursues several actions against the
nobles: he causes the publication of the civil law and the

---

[1]The new struggle is forestalled by the timely action of
the censors Quintus Fabius and Publius Decius, who put all
the humiles into four urban tribes (46.14-15). Presumably
serious discord between the nobles and the urban mob would
not break out until the time of the Gracchi.

[2]Actually the new domestic alignment began to take
shape during the censorship of Appius Claudius Caecus, who
distributed the humiles through all the tribes (46.11).
Livy, however, does not even mention this fact in his long
discussion of Claudius' censorship (29.5-30.2, 33.3-34.26).
What he does instead is to depict Claudius as an exemplum of
the worst qualities of a magistrate. Note his perverted
idea of merit (34.22): "...uirtutem in superbia, in audacia,
in contemptu deorum hominumque ponis." By ignoring the new
domestic alignment during Claudius' actual censorship, Livy
is able to place this important development into an emphatic
position at the end of the book.

calendar (46.5); dedicates a temple of Concord against their
wishes (46.6-7); and demands that recalcitrant noble youths
treat his office with proper deference (46.8-9). His provocation causes a rift in the State. Thus, even as the
plebeians and patricians are becoming reconciled, the rise
of the factio forensis and the optimate party hints at the
beginning of a new chapter of discord (46.13): "Ex eo tempore
in duas partes discessit ciuitas; aliud integer populus,
fautor et cultor bonorum, aliud forensis factio tenebat."

Events dealing with the struggle of the orders in
Books VIII and IX are not only few, they are briefly treated:
a reflection of their relative unimportance. The struggle
in 339 requires well under one page in the Teubner text, as
does the end of nexum. The episode of Gnaeus Flavius takes
slightly over one page, while the squabble at IX.26.8-22 takes
up one and one-half pages. By contrast, the conspiracy at
VII.38.5-41.8 took up four and one-half pages. Even this is
well less than the nine pages for the Manlian sedition
(VI.11, 14-20) and the nearly twelve pages on the Licinio-
Sextian Laws (VI.34-42).

BOOK X

The pentad's final book, like Books VIII and IX, deals
mostly with military events.[1] John Briscoe goes so far as to

---

[1]Briscoe in Livy, ed. T. A. Dorey (London and Toronto
1971) 18 n. 11 states that 72 percent of Book X is devoted to
military events, 28 percent to domestic events.

say, "No great events in domestic politics occur in Book X."[1]
He is wrong. In spite of the book's military character Livy
records one debate and one event which are, in his eyes, of
cardinal importance in resolving the struggle of the orders.
These are the debate on the Ogulnian Law and the quarrel of
Publius Decius Mus with his colleague Quintus Fabius. The
debate reviews the performance of plebeian consuls and vindi-
cates them as equally competent as patricians to serve in
high office. The resolution of the quarrel demonstrates a
shift in the patricians' attitude: they are willing to live
harmoniously even with plebeians who (like Decius) refuse to
take second place in serving their country. We have seen
Romans living in relative harmony ever since the orders
learned modestia and moderatio during the dictatorship of
Valerius Corvus. Now the final demonstration of the plebeians'
merit, and patricians' acceptance of their active role in
government, add a new element: mutual respect between the
orders. Henceforth, with this mutual respect as a foundation,
harmony will be established on an enduring basis.

In 300 Quintus and Gnaeus Ogulnius propose[1] to add four
plebeians to the college of pontiffs, five to the college of
augurs (6.6). The immediate issue involved in the proposal
is religious; in fact, patricians predictably object that the
sacred offices would be "profaned" (6.10: polluantur) by

---

[1]Livy, ed. T. A. Dorey (London and Toronto 1971) 1.

[2]The account of the Ogulnian Law may be found at
6.3-9.2.

plebeian membership. And yet it is clear that wider issues
are involved. They are offended by this proposal as they
were by the opening of the consulship (6.9);[1] indeed, they
raise the same objections that they brought against the
Licinian Law sixty-seven years earlier (7.2).[2] There,
patricians raised two challenges to the plebeians' holding
high office: they were not consular timber in the first
place, and were displeasing to the gods besides.

Decius' response (7.3-8.12) transcends the immediate
issue of priesthoods to address the broad and important historical issue: he asserts that plebeians have proven their
worth to the State. He cites actual historical examples of
their deeds since 367 to argue that they have demonstrated
great stature: Claudius' old objections have been disproved
by events.

Many examples prove the plebeians' worth before the
gods. The devotio of Decius' own father,[3] for example,
demonstrates that a plebeian might seem "pure and dutiful to
the immortal gods" (7.4: purum piumque deis immortalibus) no

---

[1]"...iuxta eam rem aegre passi patres quam cum consulatum uolgari uiderent."

[2]"Qui [sc. Ap. Claudius et Decius Mus] cum eadem ferme
de iure patrum ac plebis quae pro lege Licinia quondam
contraque eam dicta erant cum plebeiis consulatus rogabatur
disseruissent...". It is most unusual that Livy recognizes
explicitly the thematic connection between the two laws.
Indeed, he treats the Ogulnian Law primarily as an opportunity
to offer observations of general historical importance at
6.9-8.12. He gives only brief attention to the actual bill
(6.3-8) and its passage (9.1-2).

[3]See VIII.6.9-13 and 9.1-12.

less than any patrician (7.3-5). Further, the _vota_ of
plebeian magistrates have frequently benefited the republic
(7.6). They have also proven their worthiness in the gods'
sight by serving as decemviri sacris faciundis (8.1-4);[1] an
impressive congeries verborum underscores the important
religious functions which they discharge in this priesthood
(8.2). Lastly, he lists the emblems of distinction which
plebeians have gained by virtue of their offices or military
triumphs; surely men of such stature will reflect credit on
the priesthoods (7.9-12).

From his discussion of religious worth Decius passes
easily into a demonstration that plebeians can handle curule
office as well as patricians. After praising the efficacy
of plebeian officials' _vota_, for example, it is natural
that Decius should praise their actual deeds in office (7.7).
He concludes that plebeian commanders will enjoy equal confidence with patrician leaders in time of war (7.8). Again
the very emblems of distinction, which showed that plebeians
would credit the priesthoods, are also a proof of their
"acknowledged fitness for office" (7.12: dignatione nostra
honoris). At 8.4-11 he argues with particular force that
plebeian magistrates are fully equal in stature to patrician
ones. The patrician order has a human, not a divine, origin;
its members have no greater claim to talent than any freeborn
men (8.6, 8.10). Indeed, they are as likely to serve plebeian

---

[1]Livy recorded the plebeians' successful struggle for
this priesthood at VI.37.12 and 42.2.

magistrates as the reverse (8.5). The achievements of
plebeians, on the other hand, have brought every prize within
their grasp; he lists with pride those plebeians who first
attained the various curule magistracies (8.7-8). Plebeian
families are already building traditions of service (8.11).[1]
Decius concludes that events since 367 have proven, and will
continue to prove, that plebeians are qualified to hold the
magistracies (8.10): "aeque adhuc prosperum plebeium et
patricium fuit porroque erit."

Livy devotes his account of the Ogulnian Law, then, to
showing the progress of one of the fundamental issues in
this pentad. He clearly regards the plebeians' performance
in office since 367 as the decisive factor proving their
merit. Once a Claudius could deride the plebeians as men of
little talent, and unfit to hold the auspices. But in 300
those arguments can no longer be accepted. In Decius'
audience, Livy realizes, would be many who could remember
(7.3) the devotio of the elder Decius. How could they
believe the plebeians unfit to deal with the gods (7.4-5)?
Besides, by 300 the plebeians have established a record of
service, a tradition growing richer with each passing year
(8.11): "Consulem iam patrem ciere possum auumque iam
poterit filius meus." Success, and the passage of time, have
proved the plebeians' merit--and have freed them to help the
State (8.4): "...adiuuent uos homines plebeii diuinis quoque

---

[1]See also 7.11, where the allusion to plebeian families'
imagines, though perhaps anachronistic, at least hinted at
the growth of such traditions.

rebus procurandis, sicut in ceteris humanis pro parte uirili
adiuuant."

In spite of the debate on the Ogulnian Law, the low
level of discord which characterized Books VIII and IX seems
to continue through the first half of Book X. The Ogulnian
Law itself, to be sure, generates a certain amount of heat
between the orders (6.3-5). Yet the patricians show none of
the old fire in resisting the bill; they even expect to be
defeated (6.11).[1] Their very loss of heart seems to indicate that the struggle is approaching its final stages.[2]

Traces of strife are few in the middle of Book X. The
passage of a Valerian Law de provocatione (9.3-6) does not
occasion a heated political battle at all, though Livy does
acknowledge that it was passed to curb the power of the
patricians (9.4). Livy foregoes an obvious chance to demonstrate class strife when he records, without comment, the
aediles' fines against people who own too much land (13-14).[3]
Nor is any conflict between the orders actually recorded at
15.7-12, for it is not the plebeians but Fabius who turns
back the patricians' attempt to regain both consulships at
this time. The patricians do, however, once register their
scorn for the plebeians' merit (15.9).

---

[1] Cf. VIII.15.9.

[2] The omission of Claudius' speech against the Ogulnian
Law aids the impression that strife has diminished.

[3] Livy also notes briefly the harmony of the orders at
6.2, while at 13.8-13 all unanimously clamor that Fabius
should be consul.

There is little of significance, then, between the
Ogulnian Law and the important series of incidents at
18.5-30.10. The plebeians' worth continues to draw some
conventional fire from the patricians in spite of its clear
demonstration in Decius' speech.

Livy brings the domestic strife to a climax and apparent
conclusion with a final major conflict: the quarrel of
Decius and Fabius in 295 (24.1-30.10).[1] It is a feature of
Livy's narrative technique to conclude major historical
issues in dramatic fashion. Since the struggle of the orders
has continued in desultory fashion since the end of Book VII,
he uses two scenes to revive dramatic interest in it and its
implications. Nor is this quarrel important only as the
dramatic climax of Rome's domestic struggle. It also shows
that patricians have adopted a new attitude: they accept the
fact that plebeian magistrates are their equals in merit,
who will insist on an equal share of the rights and responsibilities of citizenship. Herein lies the key to ending
the long struggle of the orders.

The two preliminary scenes--the quarrel of Claudius and
Volumnius (18.5-19.22) and the establishment of a cult of
Pudicitia Plebeia (23.3-10)--dramatically rekindle the long

---

[1]We shall see in Chapter Two that the Samnites' military
fortunes are in steady decline for a long period. For their
decisive defeat at Sentinum, however, Livy suddenly revives
an acute sense of danger. Admittedly, there really is great
danger to Rome in this battle, since it matches a formidable
new coalition against Rome. Partly, though, the dramatic
treatment of the narrative reflects Livy's own fondness for
resolving great issues in grand fashion.

quiescent struggle[1] and make important observations on issues
involved in the contest. The quarrel of the patrician consul
Claudius and his plebeian colleague, Volumnius, which takes
place during a military campaign in Etruria, is briefly but
vividly drawn. Livy stresses here the general truth that
such internal divisions can only harm the State. Their
plan to split their armies is seen as a betrayal of the
republic (19.1-2): "Pars imperatorem suum [sc. Ap. Claudium]
orare ne collegae auxilium, quod acciendum ultro fuerit, sua
sponte oblatum sperneretur; plures abeunti Volumnio obsistere;
obtestari ne prauo cum collega certamine rem publicam
prodat...".[2] Volumnius later points out the same lesson:
that this quarrel, which briefly jeopardized Rome's safety,
demonstrates the need for absolute cooperation among officials
(22.4-5). Finally, the victory of their combined forces over
the foe shows the benefits of harmony (19.10-22).

Strife recurs when Verginia, the patrician wife of the
plebeian consul Volumnius, finds herself excluded from the
worship of Pudicitia Patricia because she has married a
plebeian (23.3-4). Livy sees in this incident a renewed
patrician challenge to the plebeians' merit.[3] She responds

---

[1]Volumnius responds with grace to Claudius' hostile words
at 18.11-14. The rancor between the two, however, appears
clearly in their orations at 19.5-9.

[2]See also 19.4: "...dimitti ab Appio eum [sc. Volumnium]
sed a re publica et ab exercitu retineri...".

[3]The institution of the cult of Pudicitia Plebeia is
mentioned in no other ancient historian. Whether this fact
is due to Livy's exceptional judgment of the episode's
importance, or simply to the accidents of survival, cannot be
known.

by citing their deeds as the proof of their worth. She has
every reason to be proud of her husband (23.5): "...nec se
uiri honorumue eius ac rerum gestarum paenitere ⟨ex⟩ uero
gloriaretur." Further, she establishes a cult of Pudicitia
Plebeia and urges plebeian women to vie with the patricians
in modesty even as their men compete in merit (23.7-8):[1]

> 'hanc ego aram' inquit 'Pudicitiae Plebeiae
> dedico; uosque hortor ut, quod certamen
> uirtutis uiros in hac ciuitate tenet, hos
> pudicitiae inter matronas sit detisque
> operam ut haec ara quam illa, si quid potest,
> sanctius et a castioribus coli dicatur.'

Livy himself endorses Verginia's determination to prove
their worth; he calls her deed "outstanding" (23.6: egregio)
and acknowledges the purity of these early plebeian worship-
ers (23.9).[2]

During the consulship of Decius and Fabius in 295,[3]
a dispute arises which brings to a head the domestic strife
and the issue of the plebeians' merit. The immediate quarrel
arises over the allotment of consular provinces: both men
want to assume command over the great and difficult war in
Etruria. Livy, however, treats it as a test of the plebeians'
worth. He emphasizes this larger implication of the episode

---

[1]This is the only explicit reference in the pentad to
the "contest of merit" which stands behind so many major
incidents in the struggle of the orders. With this idea may
be compared Sallust (Catiline 9): "...ciues cum ciuibus de
uirtute certabant...".

[2]Later the cult became polluted, and finally perished
(23.10).

[3]They served as colleagues in the consulship twice earlier,
in 308 and 297.

in two ways. First, he regards the scope allowed to Decius'
personal ambition and talent as indicative of the role allowed plebeians in the state. Second, he transposes the
consuls' personal dispute into a quarrel between the orders.

When Etruria is assigned to Fabius, Decius believes his
own talents have been slighted (24.12). He is willing to
yield to Fabius' glory--provided that his own chance for fame
is not eclipsed (24.10-11, 24.13). But beyond the honor and
the glory--which he is even willing to yield out of respect
for his colleague's age and stature--Decius cannot yield his
share of danger (24.14): "postremo se collegae honores
praemiaque concessurum uerecundia aetatis eius maiestatisque;
cum periculum, cum dimicatio proposita sit, neque cedere sua
sponte neque cessurum."

Decius speaks as a man whose father has already served
as consul, and who himself has been consul three previous
times as well as censor. His words here embody the aspira-
tions of the entire class of plebeians who now seek the
highest magistracies. Decius assumes a symbolic function;
therefore Livy draws the implications of his case in univer-
sal, not individual, terms. Decius sees the provincial
assignment as a test of the plebeians' role in the state. He
insists that men of his order have demonstrated great natural
talents (24.9): "...ipsa uirtus peruicerit ne in ullo genere
hominum inhonorata esset...". Indeed their contribution is
important if Rome is to prosper (24.17).[1]

---

[1]"certe et id natura aequum et exemplo utile esse et ad

Livy's desire to emphasize the broad implications of
this quarrel causes him also to portray it as a dispute
between the two orders, not the two magistrates. One device
to divorce them from this quarrel is that he has already
portrayed these two men as models of cooperation in earlier
chapters.[1] Livy now mentions again their tradition of concord at 24.1-2. Another device is bolder still: he simply
states that the consuls had virtually nothing to do with
their own dispute (24.2): "...ordinum magis quam ipsorum
[sc. consulum] inter se certamen interuenisse reor...".[2] Instead, he emphasizes the clash of the patrician and plebeian
classes. It is the plebeians, not Decius, who demand the
allotment of provinces by sortitio (24.2-3). Decius complains at 24.8-9 of the senate's opposition to plebeian magistrates and speaks darkly of "the power of a few" (24.9:

_____

famam populi Romani pertinere, eos consules esse quorum
utrolibet duce bellum Etruscum geri recte possit."

[1]Before their election as consuls for 297 Fabius speaks
of their proven compatibility (13.13). Their cooperative-
ness is very evident when they allot provinces according to
their skills (14.1-2). The cooperation between them, and the
importance of such cooperation, is stated most emphatically
during the election for 295 (22.2-3): "...uersa postremo
[oratio Fabi] ad collegam P. Decium poscendum: id senectuti
suae adminiculum fore. censura duobusque consulatibus simul
gestis expertum se nihil concordi collegio firmius ad rem
publicam tuendam esse, nouo imperii socio uix iam adsuescere
senilem animum posse; cum moribus notis facilius se communi-
caturum consilia." They are further said to be "of one
mind and heart" (22.6: uno animo, una mente).

[2]The attribution of the contest primarily to the orders
seems bold first, because it removes the two immediate disputants, and second, because it does not explain why the
people finally vote to assign the Etrurian command to Fabius
(24.18).

paucorum potestatem) who strive to frustrate the popular
will. Moreover, he urges the people to assert their legiti-
mate authority over their own affairs rather than to depend
on the patricians' favors (24.15).

The quarrel's resolution, however, demonstrates the
acceptance of plebeian merit by patricians. Fabius, having
proceeded to his Etrurian command, soon returns to Rome to
consult about reinforcements. Given the choice of any
commander to join him (25.17), he graciously asks Decius to
come. This action has two important effects. It symbolizes
the reconciliation not just of the two men (for the quarrel
over the provinces was not theirs), but of the patrician and
plebeian orders. Even more importantly, it shows a new basis
for the reconciliation: patricians now acknowledge that
plebeians can be fully qualified to carry out consular
duties (26.2-3):

> ...ceterum si sibi adiutorem belli sociumque
> imperii darent, quonam modo se obliuisci P.
> Deci consulis per tot collegia experti posse?
> neminem omnium secum coniungi malle et copiarum
> satis sibi cum P. Decio et nunquam nimium
> hostium fore.

Livy, then, sees in the ending of this quarrel the
resolution of a major issue which has been prominent through
the whole pentad. In 367 plebeians saw that the Licinio-
Sextian Laws would give them a chance to demonstrate their
merits as consuls. The speech of Decius on the Ogulnian Law
in 300 showed they believed their performance had proven
their worth to the State. Only now, however, do the
patricians--of whom Fabius is here the symbol--acknowledge

the merits of the plebeians. Livy sees in this episode not
only the restoration of domestic harmony, but its restoration
on an enduring basis: the mutual respect of the orders.

The narrative technique used in this episode resembles
in many ways the striking technique used to relate the military conspiracy of 342. There Quinctius was disassociated
from his march on Rome so that he could worthily embody
modestia. Here Decius and Fabius are divorced from the dispute over provinces so that the contest might be clearly seen
as one between the two orders, not just the two men. In 342
Quinctius and Valerius symbolized the attitudes of modestia
and moderatio which were adopted by the orders. Here Decius
symbolizes the plebs so that, when Etruria is denied him, it
is the worth of all plebeians which is challenged. He and
Fabius are both used symbolically in the end, where their
reconciliation on the basis of respect symbolizes the reconciliation of the orders on that basis.[1]

After the acknowledgment of the plebeians' merits, Decius
provides signal proof of their excellence in the ensuing battle at Sentinum. There he charges the Gauls along with the
bravest of his cavalry, urging them to win the victory before
Fabius (28.7). It is after this cavalry attack fails, however,
that Decius gives the greatest proof of his worth to the
State. As the Gauls begin to rout his men, Decius personally

---

[1]The symbolic use of individuals is not rare in Livy.
Examples are the centurions at II.23.2-7 and VI.14.3-8, who
symbolize the plebeians; and Manlius and the Gaul, who symbolize their respective nations at VII.9.6-10.14. See below,
95.

averts disaster by devoting himself and the enemy to the
infernal gods (28.13): "Datum hoc nostro generi est ut
luendis periculis publicis piacula simus." His devotio is
the central event of this important battle since it not only
ensures the victory of Roman arms of the left wing (29.1-7)
but signals the peripeteia on the right wing as well (29.8-11).
When after the battle the slain Decius receives the praise of
his colleague (29.18-20) and of the soldiers (30.9), he has
done more than show his own worth. He has given the supreme
proof that plebeians will indeed be second to none cum
periculum, cum dimicatio proposita sit.[1]

The quarrel of Decius and Fabius represents virtually
the end of the struggle of the orders in Books VI-X; thereafter, only a few notations pertain to it at all. Some ill
will is created among the plebeians when the booty from
their campaigns under Papirius is deposited in the Treasury;
they even suffer a war-tax in the bargain (46.5-6).[2] The
army of his colleague Carvilius, however, is soothed by a

---

[1]Livy follows sources which allow him to develop the
themes of strife and reconciliation. He rejects one source
which mentions no quarrel at all between the consuls (26.5).
Another, which he also rejects, loses the sharp focus on the
consuls' quarrel and reconciliation by adding further
disputes: Claudius against Fabius, Claudius against Decius,
and even Decius against Fabius again (26.6). For the actual
battle at Sentinum Livy rejects a source which adds more
armies on both sides (30.5-6). Perhaps this version, amidst
the clutter of additional generals and forces, loses all
focus on Decius' devotio as the decisive stroke in the victory.
The main reasons for Livy's discarding this version, however,
are that it claims an incredible number of combatants (30.5)
and that it is contradicted by the majority of writers (30.7).

[2]Papirius' army received some booty at 45.14.

share of the spoils of the victories (46.15). There is no
hint of strife between the orders when fines are imposed on
people who have occupied too much public land (47.4).[1] Thus
the harmony achieved after the quarrel of Fabius and Decius
remains unbroken through the rest of the pentad.

CONCLUSIONS

We have seen that the historical development of the
struggle of the orders has received dramatic exposition in
the second pentad. Major scenes indicate the direction of
events. The sedition of Manlius, for example, strongly
revives interest in domestic discord. The debate on the
Licinio-Sextian Laws vividly portrays discord at the end of
Book VI. Moreover, it shows the patricians' hard-line challenge to the plebeians' worth: they claim that both their
incompetence and their religious status disqualify them from
the consulship. Book VII shows much progress towards re-
lieving this state of affairs. The patricians' attitude is
softened and changed in a great scene at the end of the book:
the reconciliation after the military conspiracy of 342.
Here, the selection of Valerius Publicola to compose the
sedition indicates the patricians' new willingness to act with
moderatio; for their part, the plebeians act with modestia.
In this new, tranquil atmosphere, domestic problems are
little evident in Books VIII and IX. Book X, however, resolves

---

[1]There is also a squabble at 37.6-12, but it is not
clearly between the patricians and plebeians.

the debate on the plebeians' merits and, at least in large
degree, brings the struggle of the orders to an amicable
conclusion. Debate on the Ogulnian Law, early in the book,
conclusively demonstrates the competence of plebeian magistrates. Finally, the quarrel of Decius and Fabius in the
middle of the book demonstrates a shift in the patricians'
attitude: they are willing to live harmoniously even with
plebeians who insist upon a full role in the government.
This new attitude marks a major breakthrough in relations
between the orders; it fittingly climaxes a historical
movement that has been developed through the entire pentad.

CHAPTER TWO

MILITARY EXPANSION

INTRODUCTION

The other major historical theme of Books VI-X is the
expansion of Rome's power. Although Rome enjoys military
successes in the first pentad, the Gallic sack at the end of
Book V marks a "clean break" between pentads on this issue.
So reduced is her condition after the sack that the city must
be "refounded" (VI.1.3). As we noted earlier,[1] however, the
end of Book V stirringly challenges Rome to greatness (54.7):
"Hic Capitolium est, ubi quondam capite humano inuento
responsum est eo loco caput rerum summamque imperii fore...".
As Book VI begins Rome starts anew on her expansionary
course.

The phases of the military theme, like those of the
struggle of the orders, are carefully defined in the second
pentad to show the significant stages of Rome's growth. The
salient feature of the military account is that it pivots
around the center of the pentad. First, the bestowal of
citizenship on the Latin states is impressively recounted in
the middle of Book VIII. Speeches fully indicate the
necessity of extending citizenship if Rome's empire is to
endure. The conquest of the Latins, and the decision to

---

[1]See above, 32.

grant citizenship to them, marks the end of the "local" phase of Roman conquest. Immediately, the second half of Book VIII begins with the Second Samnite War. At its outset the Samnites challenge Rome to fight for Italian hegemony. Therefore, Rome's next phase of conquest begins immediately after the first ends.

During the first half of the pentad there is no dramatic framework to indicate the importance of events. There are, to be sure, a number of engagements; some of these are related very dramatically in themselves. Taken together, however, they have no cumulative effect, for Livy never indicates that they have any larger importance. Consequently, they build towards no objective, and create no dramatic "tempo."

Immediately at the outset of the Second Samnite War, however, Livy indicates that the issue at stake is the hegemony of Italy. Military events thereafter draw their dramatic power from their connection with this overall scheme. Indeed, Livy portrays Rome's military history as a virtually unbroken string of successes through the pentad's latter half. This dramatic impression is particularly strong at the ends of Books VIII, IX, and X, which all portray Rome's forces surging forward to victory.

Livy supplements the pentad's dramatic "movement" towards greater Roman power by placing a major thematic statement of the sources of Rome's military strength at the very center of Books VI-X. Book VIII is unified around this topic.

Aside from generous treatment of allies, this book also identifies military discipline as a particular source of Roman
strength. The importance of generous treatment of allies and
of military discipline is indicated by pairs of scenes,
balanced against each other structurally as well as thematically within the book. The resulting moral statement is
important to Livy's overall conception of Rome's military
expansion; for this reason he places it at the center of the
pentad.

BOOKS VI AND VII

Aside from the lack of an interpretive schema, we may
advance another reason for the lack of dramatic emphasis, in
Books VI and VII, on Rome's military fortunes. These books
deal mostly with domestic politics. John Briscoe records
that only 43 percent of Book VI, and 57 percent of Book VII,
deal with military affairs; Books VIII, IX, and X respec-
tively devote 70, 74, and 72 percent to military affairs.[1]
Furthermore, at least before the outbreak of hostilities
with the Samnites (VII.29 ff.), these wars consist of
individual campaigns directed now against the Volsci, Latins,
or Hernici, now against some local combination of Rome's
foes. While certain of these battles may be impressively
narrated, there is little apparent connection among the
various campaigns since they lack a single military objective
upon which Livy can fix his attention.

---

[1]Livy, ed. T. A. Dorey (London and Toronto 1971) 18 n. 11.

The sundry wars of these two books do, however, show
that Rome is militarily strong. We may therefore attribute
to them this development at least: that Rome recovers[1] from
the Gallic sack of Book V and from the contempt in which her
neighbors hold her at the beginning of Book VI.[2]

Although Roman territory remains subject to frequent
raids as late as Book VII,[3] Rome's strength is yet apparent
in her many victories in Books VI and VII. At VI.7.1-8.10
the Romans crush a coalition of Latins, Hernici, and Volsci
at Satricum; at 7.3-6 Camillus even reminds the Romans of
their innate superiority over their foes. At 12.6-13.6
another great victory is won over a massive army of Volsci,
reinforced by Latins, Hernici, and people from Circeii and
Velitrae; the dictator Aulus Cornelius Cossus tells his
troops that they "are going to engage their inferiors"
(12.8: cum imparibus manus conserturos).[4] The example of
Tusculum at 25.1-26.8 shows that the surest defense against
Roman arms is nonresistance.[5] The Romans even reverse their

---

[1]See VI.1.3.

[2]See VI.2.4, 2.9.

[3]For example, VI.21.8, 27.11-28.2, 36.1; VII.12.5-6,
15.11. We also see Rome as weak or in danger: for example,
VI.2.2-4, 10.6-9, 21.2-3, 21.9; VII.25.5-7. At VI.12.2-6
Livy speaks with wonderment of the persistence of Rome's
enemies. Livy makes no attempt to balance Rome's perils
against her victories in order to draw a composite picture of
her strength.

[4]Rome's superiority is prominent also in the description
of the battle at 13.1-2.

[5]See 25.6, and especially 26.1.

earlier disgrace at the Allia.[1] The Praenestini, choosing to
fight the Romans there, calculate that the very place will
cause a rout similar to the one which the Gauls inflicted
there (28.5-6). The Romans, however, see the battle as an
opportunity to expunge their recent shame; they would conquer,
even if the Gauls themselves were present (29.8-9). The
result of the engagement matches the Romans' claim; by rout-
ing the Praenestini in the first charge (29.1-3) they do
expunge their earlier disgrace.[2] Yet another victory is won
later over the Latins and Volsci. After the surrender of
their allies the Latins, borne headlong by madness, are
destroyed to the last man at Tusculum (32.4-33.12).[3]

The account of Rome's victories in Book VI receives a
measure of unity from the dominating presence of Camillus.
He is prominent in many of Rome's most important victories.
At 2.5-4.3 he defeats the Volsci, Aequi and Etruscans; at
6.3-8.10 he receives charge over his fellow consular tri-
bunes and, as noted above, defeats a coalition of Latins,
Hernici, and Volsci; at 9.1-10.6 he recovers Sutrium and
Nepete from the Etruscans; at 22.6-24.11 he alone turns

---

[1]For the Gauls' victory over the Romans at the Allia,
see V.37.1-38.10.

[2]Note again the assertion of the Romans' superiority
over the foe (28.7). Furthermore, at 29.1-2 the Praenestini
rely on the fortune of the place while the Romans depend on
martial valor; note also the enemy's fear and the ease with
which Rome captures their towns (29.5-6).

[3]Note that the Latins are unable to inflict harm upon
the Romans (33.4).

imminent defeat into glorious victory over the Volsci; at
25.1-26.8 he handles Tusculan nonresistance with great
finesse; and at 42.4-8 he gains an easy victory over the
Gauls.[1] Livy rightly judges (1.4) that he helps to establish
in Book VI the city which he restored in Book V.[2]

Appearing in the narrative as Rome's greatest citizen,
Camillus often functions as a reminder of Rome's strength.
At 6.17, for example, Publius Valerius tells the Roman
senate that their hopes for success in war cannot exceed
their confidence in Camillus. Indeed, his presence does
prove decisive in the ensuing battle (8.5-6). It may therefore be considered an affirmation of Rome's recovery that
Livy so strongly emphasizes Camillus' glory in one of the
book's most important battles (22.6-24.11). This battle, a
stylized tour de force, deserves examination. The Romans,
under Camillus and Lucius Furius Medullinus, engage the
Volsci at the latter's insistence. Faring ill at first, they
are rallied by Camillus and win the victory. Livy, essaying
to glorify Camillus, portrays him before the peripeteia as
old and correspondingly prudent, infinitely wiser than the
rash Medullinus.[3] Furthermore, Camillus is carefully

---

[1]He also serves briefly as dictator in a civil quarrel
(38.3-13).

[2]For the opinion of Camillus' fellows, see, for
example, 6.6-7 and 38.3-4. See also Livy's final verdict
at VII.1.10.

[3]On Camillus' age see 22.7, 23.4-7, 23.9, 23.11, and
24.5. On his prudence see 23.1 and the later reference at
24.9. On Medullinus' rashness see 22.6 and 23.3-8; he later
admits his temerity at 24.9. The combination of a prudent

disassociated from the unfortunate decision to engage the
foe.[1] After he intervenes to restore Rome's fortunes at
24.5, however, we find a completely different portrayal of
both men. Again Camillus is glorified at the expense of his
colleague, but now he is a vigorous leader;[2] a chastened
Medullinus learns that his station is to follow his betters.[3]
We should note that the dynamic Camillus of 24.5-7 cannot be
reconciled with the elderly one of 22.7-24.5. Indeed, Livy
exploits the contrast for effect. At 23.11 Camillus begs not
to be stationed in the front line on the score of age; at
24.5 he must actually be lifted by his attendants into the
saddle.[4] Yet no sooner has he mounted than, casting aside
his years, he calls up the reserves, vigorously chides his
men, and even risks his life in the front line (24.5-7). The
metamorphosis in Camillus at 24.5-7 not only coincides with
the reversal in the battle but even produces the reversal,

---

commander with a rash one was a topos of military history:
for example, Fabius with Minucius and Aemilius with Varro in
Book XXII.

[1]See 22.6, 23.9-11, 24.5, 24.9, 25.3-4, 25.6, and
especially 23.12.

[2]See 24.5-7.

[3]See 24.8-9 and 25.3.

[4]This is a variation, which enhances the tour de force,
on one of Livy's favored motifs. He often includes touches
of energetic physical action, such as leaping onto or down
from a horse, to add to the vigorous effect of a scene: for
example, VII.33.9, VIII.9.9 and IX.31.10. Camillus himself
provides the best example of the motif. In spite of his
advancing years (VI.8.2) he leaps onto his horse (7.3) to
give a speech; having spoken, he immediately leaps down
again (8.1) to charge the enemy.

for it causes the moral recovery of the Roman troops at
24.5-10.[1] Livy has therefore created a double peripeteia:
one within Camillus, which brings about the second one within
the battle itself. He has sacrificed verisimilitude in the
portrayal of Camillus in order to achieve a forcible peripeteia and, more importantly, a double glorification of the
commander. Not only does Camillus fare well by his twofold
comparison with Medullinus, but he is portrayed as the central figure in a major Roman victory.[2]

By its victories and by the dominating figure of
Camillus, then, Book VI shows Rome's strength. Book VII
continues to demonstrate Rome's strength. At 6.1-6 the
example of Marcus Curtius, who rides fully armed into a chasm,
shows that Rome's martial valor constitutes her chief
reliance.[3] By a major victory over the Hernici at 7.1-8.7
the Romans avenge an earlier defeat. The victory illustrates
their superiority over the foe: both sides field their full
armed might;[4] furthermore, the battle becomes strictly a

---

[1]The recovery on the battlefield is merely a reflection
of this underlying moral recovery, to which Livy devotes
most of his attention. Having described the moral effect
of Camillus' vigor upon the soldiers (24.10), he describes
the rout of the Volsci and the aftermath of the battle in
just one sentence (24.11).

[2]This emphasis on Camillus is reinforced by several
references to his peerless talent for command: 22.9, 23.9,
and 24.6.

[3]See especially 6.2-3.

[4]The Romans have two armies; against them are ranged
all the Hernici of military age, including eight elite
cohorts (7.3-6).

contest between the best men of each nation (8.1); lastly, it is the accustomed fortune of each people which at length turns the battle decisively in Rome's favor (28.4). Livy's account of the single combat of Titus Manlius and the Gaul (9.6-10.14) shows a deliberate effort to emphasize Rome's military superiority over the Gauls. His narrative, apparently based on an earlier account by Claudius Quadrigarius,[1] stresses Roman supremacy in war more than Claudius did. In Livy, not only does Manlius' foe state that the combat will prove the relative fighting abilities of the two nations (9.8), but each combatant is portrayed as typical of his people. Manlius is of but average size, armed rather with useful weapons than showy ones, spurning idle exultation to reserve his ferocity for combat (10.7-8). The Gaul is enormously tall, resplendent with garb of various colors and weapons engraved with gold (10.7). He leaps before the standards (10.3) and even sticks out his tongue in derision (10.5). In actual combat, however, the Gaul slashes with great noise but little effect (10.9); Manlius, fitted for close combat (10.5), quickly dispatches him with two thrusts (10.10). Livy sees the victory as a triumph of the Roman character and Roman method of fighting over the Gallic. More victories follow. At 12.7-15.8 Livy emphasizes the Romans' military zeal which, though absent from the initial stages of battle, yet proves decisive in a great victory

---

[1]Claudius' version is preserved in Aulus Gellius IX.13.7-19. A detailed comparison of the two accounts may be found in Luce, Livy 224-226.

over the Gauls.[1] In order to portray this zeal favorably,
he has adopted a surprisingly apologetic tone towards the
soldiers' earlier eager demands for battle.[2] The appeal of
the Caerites (20.1-8) shows clearly Rome's prosperity and
her power in war. At 23.1-24.9 Roman troops defeat the
Gauls, first repelling an uphill attack, then putting to
flight their remaining forces on level ground. Finally, the
victory of Valerius Corvus over a Gaul in single combat
shows divine favor for Rome's cause and anticipates victory
over the entire Gallic force (26.6-9).[3]

The outbreak of the first Samnite War replaces Rome's
scattered successes with the pentad's first systematic
account of her success in a major war. Recognizing the
importance of these events, Livy introduces the war with a
special preface (29.1-7) and devotes to the year 343 over
nine chapters describing the course of the war.[4] Three great
victories during the year mark the success of Roman arms
against the Samnites. At 33.5-18 they gain a rout after

---

[1]See 15.1-3. Cf. 14.6: "Dictator...magis animis quam
uiribus fretus ad certamen descenderet...". A stratagem
(14.6-10) also aids in the victory at 15.5.

[2]See 12.12-13.1, etc. Though Livy normally condemns
such actions as rash or insubordinate, here he legitimizes
the soldiers' demands by the character of their spokesman,
Sextus Tullius. He is a distinguished primipilus (13.1),
most obedient to authority (13.2), mindful still of military
discipline and a commander's dignity (14.2). Even so, Livy
cannot completely excuse the army's conduct (14.1).

[3]Note that the consul Lucius Furius Camillus brings
to the fight his father's accustomed success against Gauls
(25.10-12).

[4]The first twenty-eight chapters of Book VII, by
contrast, covered twenty-three years, 366-344.

bitter struggle, while at 34.1-37.3 they turn a difficult
situation into a glorious victory. These two disasters cause
the Samnites to mass their whole strength and pin their hopes
upon a "final encounter" (37.4: certamine ultimo). And yet
they fare no better here, suffering the destruction of part
of their army, the dispersal of the rest, and the loss of
their camp (37.4-17). That Rome has virtually won the war is
clear (38.1-2): perceiving Rome's fortunes, the Falisci seek
a treaty; the Latins abandon plans to revolt; and the
Carthaginians send an embassy bearing their congratulations
and the gift of a golden crown.[1] The First Samnite War shows
Rome's military success, then, in the course of a whole war
rather than in isolated incidents.

The First Samnite War has yet another significance; it
marks Rome's first intervention beyond central Italy.[2] The
Campanian delegates, in appealing for assistance against the
Samnites, point out that Rome, by intervening, will extend
her rule into Campania and gain a strategic position behind
the Aequi and Volsci (30.7-8). The idea is echoed at 30.10,
30.18-19, and 31.1. Though Rome's expansion is undeniable,
however, it little influences the dramatic pace of the

---

[1]During the following year, 342, the Samnites are quiet
(39.1). They end the war, without any further fighting, in
341 (VIII.1.7-2.4).

[2]29.1: "Maiora iam hinc bella et uiribus hostium et
longinquitate uel regionum uel temporum [spatio] quibus
bellatum est dicentur." Livy is acutely aware that this
conflict stands at the beginning of a long series of wars,
extending far into the future, which will see a tremendous
expansion of Rome's power (29.1-2).

ensuing military narrative. The Campanians' original proposition, that Rome will extend her rule, is neither foreshadowed nor stated with the dramatic force that marks the
importance of the Samnite challenge for Italian hegemony at
VIII.23. Indeed, the several references to Roman expansion
most clearly serve a moral purpose, for they ultimately
show that Rome resists the temptation to intervene for any
save the noblest reasons.[1] We may further observe that it is
the Campanian deditio, not the fighting of 343, which extends
Roman power into Campania.[2] It is therefore unsurprising
that we do not find, in the narrative of the war itself, any
attempt to show a pattern of growing expansion into Campania.
For example, the posting of a garrison in the area at the
end of 343 (38.4) does not dramatically stress an increase
in Rome's hold on the region. The lack of any momentum in
the events is reflected also in the ending of Book VII.
Here the final scene stresses the resolution of civil quarrels, not military success. During the strong tempos of
expansion in Books VIII, IX, and X, a major victory is always
described near the end of the books to reinforce the dramatic
effect of conquest.

The first Samnite War, then, in spite of its elaborate
preface and detailed narrative, has little share in the
dramatic portrayal of Rome's expansion. Its function, in

---

[1]See below, 99.

[2]Already before the outbreak of hostilities the Senate
refers to the land as Roman property (31.9).

fact, is quite different: to emphasize the righteousness of
Rome's entry into the war and to delineate the character of
the combatants, especially the Samnites.

The lengthy account (30.1-31.12) of the Campanian embassy to Rome, the deliberations of the Roman Senate, and
the reaction of the Samnites justifies Rome's declaration of
war at 32.1. The Campanians point out that Rome may
legitimately undertake an alliance with them without violating their previous alliance with the Samnites (30.4). They
further stress the Samnites' immorality: their cruel depredations and bloodthirsty slaughter of armies; to declare
war would be righteous (30.11-17).[1] The Romans' morality,
moreover, is vindicated by their rejection of the Campanians'
appeals to the utility of intervention (31.1-2).[2] Only their
deditio allows Rome to intervene justly (31.7): "Tum iam
fides agi uisa deditos non prodi; nec facturum aequa
Samnitium populum censebant, si agrum urbemque per deditionem
factam populi Romani oppugnarent." Rome's moral position is
then reinforced by the Samnites' disdainful rejection of a
final bid for peace (31.11-12).[3]

_____

[1]30.17: "Non loquor apud recusantem iusta bella
populum...". Cf. 30.11. Their pathetic appeal at 30.21-22
also underscores the justice of intervention. The speech
greatly resembles that of the Corcyraeans in Thucydides
(I.32 ff.); see Ogilvie, Comm. 17. The speech is analyzed
by Walsh, Livy 224-225.

[2]For the Campanians' appeals to utilitas, see 30.6-8,
30.10, and 30.18-19.

[3]Note also the general emphasis on the Samnites'
injustice (29.4, 31.3, and VIII.2.1-2).

The character especially of the Samnite foe is brought forth clearly in the programmatic first battle of the war (33.5-18).[1] Livy indicates that both sides are taking each other's measure (33.5-6); the battle itself is said to reveal their respective characters (33.7). Throughout the contest the Samnites display immense tenacity. A cavalry charge fails to turn an even struggle in Rome's favor. Later, when the consul's own example fires the Romans to press forward, still the Samnites do not give ground, though they begin to take the heavier casualties. They refuse to retreat even when their fortunes turn decisively sour, so fixed is their resolve not to yield (33.13). Only the Romans' renewed fury finally turns the battle into a rout (33.14-15). The victors, however, confess that they have never fought with a more tenacious foe (33.16): "Et Romani fatebantur nunquam cum pertinaciore hoste conflictum...". The Samnites, for their part, confess that it was the Romans' blazing anger which put them to flight.

By delineating the Samnite character and the morality of Rome's intervention, the events of 343 form an introductory statement to the whole series of Samnite wars. The programmatic battle of 33.5-18 indicates the Samnite character more for the whole sequence of wars than for the war at hand. Their tenacity is evident only in the long series

---

[1] A similar device is found at XXI.29.1-4, where the first engagement of the Second Punic War is programmatic of the fortunes of the entire war: the Romans win, but only after a long struggle and heavy casualties.

of conflicts, for this is a quality which the Samnites display mainly in the persistence with which they wage war.[1] Likewise, the vindication of Rome's morality justifies not only their intervention here but also their involvement in the later Samnite wars. Although Livy portrays the Samnites as responsible for the second and third wars, he describes their guilt less fully there.[2] Since he has established Rome's righteousness here, he does not need to emphasize the idea later.

Considering its elaborate preface and detailed narrative, then, the First Samnite War has surprisingly little dramatic importance in its own right. Its function in Livy's presentation is to introduce general issues concerning the greater wars which follow.

BOOK VIII

Standing at the center of the pentad, Book VIII serves as the pivot of the entire military narrative. At the end of the first half of the book and pentad, Livy portrays the consolidation of Rome's power by the grant of citizenship to several neighboring states. Immediately, Rome is able to strike out in the logical next step to extend her power: the domination of Italy. This issue occupies the second half of the book and the rest of the pentad.

---

[1] See X.31.10-15. Neither in Book VII nor later do the Samnites achieve much success against the Romans on a fair battlefield.

[2] VIII.23.1-9, X.11.11-12.2.

Aside from portraying the ongoing process of Rome's
expansion, however, Book VIII portrays Rome learning two important things: generosity to allies and a new form of
military discipline which recognizes the dignity of her
soldiers. Livy sees Rome's military success as the result,
in no small measure, of her mastery of these moral qualities.
While citizenship has been granted to certain towns before,
it is only in Book VIII that Livy shows the Romans at a
crossroads: they must decide, as a matter of general policy,
whether to rule by kindness or terror. Their choice of the
former is said to strengthen their empire; it immediately
makes possible further military expansion. Beyond wise
statesmanship, Rome now learns in two scenes that unmiti-
gated severitas is not as effective a mode of discipline as
the more humane treatment of soldiers. This realization is
likewise part of Rome's growth; it represents a clear development up from the city's rude beginnings. The rough-and-
ready types--vagabonds, exiles, shepherds--who formed the
early city needed, perhaps, to be held in check by force.[1]
Modestia and moderatio were ideals seldom in evidence for
long in Books I-V; no sooner did one party yield than the
other took advantage.[2] Far different are the citizens of

_____

[1]See II.1.4-5. There are, of course, examples of
moderatio even among the commanders of early Rome; see, for
example, II.60.1-3. On the development of national character
in early Rome see Luce, Livy 241-249.

[2]For example, III.65.7. See Livy's verdict on the era
(III.65.11): "Adeo moderatio tuendae libertatis, dum aequari
uelle simulando ita se quisque extollit ut deprimat alium, in
difficili est, cauendoque ne metuant, homines metuendos

this era. The growth of civic virtue is nowhere more evident
than in the domestic harmony which, as we have seen, has already begun to pervade the State. In this more civilized
nation, Livy shows in Book VIII that a more humane form of
discipline is far more effective in creating military success
than the harshness of antiquity.

Book VIII thus demonstrates a great thematic concentra-
tion on the expansion of Rome's military power and the moral
qualities behind the expansion. To show the book's thematic
unity I shall digress somewhat from the order of exposition
followed elsewhere. Instead of treating scenes in order, I
shall first cover two pairs of scenes: grants of citizenship
followed by the challenge to Italian hegemony; then (on military discipline) the imperium Manlianum and the quarrel of
Fabius and Decius. We may note here the careful architec-
tural balance creates a formal centerpiece for the entire
pentad;[1] at the focal point are the expansion of Rome's
power, and the moral qualities behind the expansion. This
mode of emphasis accords with Livy's methods elsewhere. In
the first pentad, for example, he fixed the Decemvirate as
the central pivot (III.33 ff.);[2] in the seventh pentad it is
the proclamation of the freedom of Greece (XXXIII.32 ff.).[3]

---

ultro se efficiunt, et iniuriam ab nobis repulsam, tamquam
aut facere aut pati necesse sit, iniungimus aliis."

[1]No other book in the pentad evidences the close
thematic unity or structural design of Book VIII.

[2]Burck, Erzählungskunst 8.

[3]Luce, Livy 33.

Finally, I will examine the other scenes of Book VIII.
We shall find that, to emphasize Rome's expansion, the
dramatic pace of the military narrative rises to a climax at
the end of this book.

Among the strictures aimed at Livy's history is his
failure to comprehend the significance of historical change.
Walsh levels this charge against him regarding the extension
of citizenship to the allies. He says that "a comparison of
the two accounts [sc. in Livy and Dionysius] of the extension
of citizenship to Tusculum in 381 clearly suggests that
Dionysius was far more aware of its significance in the growth
of Roman dominion than was Livy."[1] Nothing could be further
from the truth. The complaint illustrates the danger of
reaching general conclusions about Livy's historical interpretation by examining only particular scenes. True, Livy
does not point out the significance of the specific grant of
citizenship to Tusculum.[2] He has not ignored the entire
issue, however; he has merely deferred detailed treatment of
its significance until the Latin Rebellion in Book VIII.[3]

---

[1] Walsh, Livy 164. With Livy VI.26.8 compare Dionysius
XIV.6.

[2] Livy also refrains from detailed treatment of the
grant of citizenship to certain Veientes, Capenates, and
Faliscans (VI.4.4). He treats this act as only a minor
illustration of Rome's recovery from the Gallic sack.

[3] Livy has recognized the importance of admitting new
citizens from the time of the city's founding. Romulus'
grant of asylum to the rabble of neighboring peoples was
important as a first step in the city's growth (I.8.4-7).
Even more important in securing Rome's future greatness,
however, was the Rape of the Sabine women (I.9.1-3): "Iam

By treating it where he does, in fact, Livy is able to point
out its historical significance most fully. In Livy, debate
on the extension of citizenship coincides with the point
where Rome decisively commits herself to broad grants of
citizenship. Further, her decision brings immediate and
important results: a wider expansion of Roman power. It
is Livy's presentation, not Dionysius',[1] which points out
the historical significance of the events in a dramatic way.

As Rome completes her conquest of the rebellious Latins
in 338 (VIII.13-14), Livy deals only briefly with the great
victories which forced their submission.[2] He concentrates
instead on the formation of a lasting confederation with the
Latins.[3]

---

res Romana adeo erat ualida ut cuilibet finitimarum
ciuitatium bello par esset; sed penuria mulierum hominis
aetatem duratura magnitudo erat...urbes quoque, ut cetera,
ex infimo nasci; dein, quas sua uirtus ac di iuuent, magnas
opes sibi magnumque nomen facere...". Moreover, Livy at
least notes that the bestowal of citizenship on the whole
Sabine people (I.13.4-5) and on the Albans (I.30.1) each
doubled the population. Further grants of citizenship are
also said to foster the city's growth at I.33.1-9.

[1] It is impossible to reconstruct the effect of
Dionysius' account, which survives for this period only in
excerpts. Even the order of these excerpts is often open to
question. His complete narrative from the earlier books,
however, evinces little evidence of dramatic control to
rival Livy; see Walsh, Livy 230-231. Admittedly Dionysius,
like Livy, brings out the Romans' generosity in obtaining
the lasting friendship of Privernum (XIV.13).

[2] Two major victories in pitched battles, plus a successful campaign to reduce the cities of Latium, are all related
at 13.4-8. These victories earned the consuls not only the
right to triumph, but to have their equestrian statues
placed in the Forum (13.9).

[3] The Latins earlier touched on the issue of a stable
association with Rome, but on unacceptable terms: complete
political equality (4.1-5.6).

A speech by the consul L. Furius Camillus (13.11-18)
sets forth the important issue: Rome's policy towards her
quondam allies will determine the durability of her rule and
her military strength. After proclaiming the rebellion
crushed (13.11-12), he states that the task at hand must be
to ensure lasting peace (13.13): "Reliqua consultatio est,
quoniam rebellando saepius nos sollicitant, quonam modo
perpetua pace quietos obtineamus." He then outlines the
alternatives for achieving peace: be clement to the Latins or
destroy them utterly (13.14).[1] Harsh treatment of the Latins,
however, will merely weaken Rome's military power; Camillus
points out that they have supplied many troops (13.15). By
contrast clemency, their ancestors' traditional policy, offers two advantages. It will allow the Roman state, and its
power, to increase. Further, it will place their rule on an
enduring foundation (13.16): "Voltis exemplo maiorum augere
rem Romanam uictos in ciuitatem accipiendo? materia cres-
cendi per summam gloriam suppeditat. Certe id firmissimum
longe imperium est quo oboedientes gaudent."

The Roman senate responds to his speech by deciding to
treat each vanquished people individually (14.1-2). Livy
recites the terms granted various peoples at length (14.2-12);
several are granted some degree of citizenship, while others
are specially punished on grounds of extended or serious

---

[1]See also 13.17: "illorum animos...seu poena seu
beneficio praeoccupari oportet." Cf. IX.3.4-13 where the
Samnites, facing the same choice, decide to be harsh--to
their cost.

offenses and yet others are specially rewarded for their ser-
vices. Fairness is the order of the day; Rome's conduct earns
the gratitude of the conquered (15.1). It is clear that the
senate has indeed established that kind of authority which
the Latins shall willingly obey.

Rome's fairness towards her dependent cities is again
apparent in a minor incident at 19.9-13. A war with
Privernum, whose forces are under the command of Vitruvius
Vaccus of Fundi, causes the Roman leader Plautius to lead
his army against Fundi. Yet the senate of that town success-
fully petitions him to spare its innocent population.[1]

The issue of creating a lasting alliance recurs at
20.10-21.10, after the defeat of Privernum. While the
Roman senate debates whether to deal harshly or kindly with
the people of Privernum, one of the Privernian legates boldly
proclaims his unwavering devotion to liberty (21.1-2). Under
questioning, he asserts that only a just peace can last; un-
fair terms will soon be repudiated.[2]

Some senators, advocating harshness, denounce the legate
for making threats and inciting another rebellion (21.5).

---

[1]Livy notes, but does not adopt, a variant from Claudius
Quadrigarius which recorded considerably harsher treatment
of the Fundani (19.13-14).

[2]21.3-4: "Cuius [sc. legati Priuernatis] cum feroci
responso infestiores factos uideret consul eos qui ante
Priuernatium causam impugnabant, ut ipse benigna interro-
gatione mitius responsum eliceret, 'quid si poenam' inquit
'remittimus uobis, qualem nos pacem uobiscum habituros
speremus?' 'Si bonam dederitis,' inquit 'et fidam et
perpetuam; si malam, haud diuturnam.'"

Yet those prevail who admire[1] his words as those of a free

man. Mindful of their recent lesson on moderate rule, they

acknowledge that peace can be faithfully observed only where

it is willingly embraced, not where slavery is imposed.[2] The

senate ultimately grants citizenship to the Privernians, on

the principle that men whose only thought is for liberty are

worthy to be Romans (21.8-10). By this action the senate

confirms the Roman commitment to maintaining a firm peace,

and a lasting alliance.[3]

We should note that the effectiveness of this scene

depends on the belief that the Privernians can be turned into

loyal supporters of Rome. Livy, however, faces a difficulty

in presenting them in this way. At 19.10-14 even the innoc-

uous Fundani were suspected of disloyalty. Far more,

therefore, ought the Privernians to be suspected, for they

have actually revolted.[4] To eliminate any nagging doubt

about their disloyalty, Livy has the consul Plautius simply

---

[1] Livy clearly indicates his sympathy for the position
of the Privernian legate. His pithy sententiae at 21.2 and
21.4 show a spirited love of freedom. He is characterized
as mindful of his free birth rather than his present mis-
fortune (21.1). Finally, the pars melior senatus (or, with
Duker, pars mitior senatus) yields to his wisdom (21.6).

[2] 21.6-7: "pars melior senatus ad molliora responsa
trahere et dicere uiri et liberi uocem auditam; an credi posse
ullum populum aut hominem denique in ea condicione, cuius eum
paeniteat, diutius quam necesse sit mansurum? ibi pacem esse
fidam ubi uoluntarii pacati sint, neque eo loco ubi seruitutem
esse uelint, fidem sperandam esse."

[3] As at 13.15-16, there is an indication of the
alliance's military usefulness: it will strengthen Rome's
hand against the Samnites (20.12).

[4] The Fundani were quick to point this out (19.11).

dismiss the question of general complicity in the defection.
He limits the blame to a few and flatly asserts the inno-
cence of the people at large (20.10-11).[1] The Privernians
who emerge from Livy's account are not false friends but
noble lovers of freedom, worthy to be Romans, whose support
is greatly to be prized.

Thus Livy has carefully drawn the creation of the
system of allies and has shown that it ensures Rome's military greatness. Enduring peace with Latins marks the com-
pletion of the "local" phase of Roman conquest.

The "national" phase of conquest begins immediately,
with a renewal of hostilities with the Samnites. As with
Rome's other great wars, an introductory sketch traces the
background of the conflict (22.5-10): the origin and history
of the people of Palaepolis-Neapolis, their aggression
against the Romans in the regions of Campania and Falerii,
the Samnites' ambiguous attitude towards their alliance with
Rome and apparent readiness to repudiate it upon word of a
Campanian defection, Rome's righteous declaration of war
upon Palaepolis, and the division of consular provinces.

At 23.1-10, a passage unfortunately broken off by a
lacuna, dramatic tension rises to a peak. At first there
is "little hope for peace" (23.1: _exiguam_ _spem_ _pacis_) as
the Samnites' preparations for war are reported (23.1-2).

---

[1]Plautius speaks with an authority exactly like that of
the _legati_ of VIII.32.14-18. See below, 119, 123. As the
legati speak authoritatively there, so Livy intends the
reader to accept Plautius' interpretation of the Privernians'
actions here: they are innocent rather than guilty.

Then, a Roman delegation is rebuffed: the Samnites fiercely
deny allegations of wrongdoing, and inveigh against the
Roman actions. They avow their readiness to fight, and
demand that Rome abandon the colony of Fregellae (23.3-7).
Finally, when the Romans propose further discussion,[1] the
Samnites propose to let the sword resolve their disputes
(23.8-9).[2] More importantly, the Samnites emphatically mark
off a new phase in Rome's conquests. Henceforth, the issue
at stake in their struggle will be the hegemony of Italy
(23.8-9):

> ...'quid perplexe agimus?' inquit [Samnis
> quidam]; 'nostra certamina, Romañi, non
> uerba legatorum nec hominum quisquam
> disceptator sed campus Campanus, in quo
> concurrendum est, et arma et communis Mars
> belli decernet. Proinde inter Capuam
> Suessulamque castra castris conferamus et
> Samnis Romanusne imperio Italiam regat
> decernamus.'

The dramatic thesis, that peninsular dominion is at issue in
the war, is reiterated at 27.2-4. There the Tarentines
perceive, to their alarm, that victory over the Samnites
will make Rome mistress of Italy:

> ...ira atque inuidia in Romanos [Tarentini]
> furere, eo etiam quod Lucanos et Apulos
> --nam utraque eo anno societas coepta est--
> in fidem populi Romani uenisse allatum est:

---

[1]The Samnites' bellicose tone, combined with the Romans'
conciliatory attitude, marks the Samnites as morally responsible for the war.

[2]According to Madvig, Emendationes Livianae
(Copenhagen 1860) ad loc. war is about to be declared when
the lacuna interrupts. He believes that we have lost the
end of the narrative dealing with Rome's legation to the
Samnites, the declaration of war against them, the beginning
of the siege of Naples, and perhaps more.

> quippe propemodum peruentum ad se esse
> iamque in eo rem fore ut Romani aut hostes
> aut domini habendi sint. discrimen profecto
> rerum suarum in bello Samnitium euentuque
> eius uerti; eam solam gentem restare nec eam
> ipsam satis ualidam, quando Lucanus defecerit....

As Rome stands on the threshold of her greatest war to
date, these small "touches" set up the thematic scheme
governing events to follow. The long account of the struggle,
great in itself, indicates the importance which Livy assigns
to its outcome.[1] Most of all, however, it is this
dramatic thesis which tells the reader that Rome is involved
in her greatest fight, in which the winner will receive lord-
ship of Italy; the loser, eternal subjugation.

The mid-point of the pentad, then, is the pivot of the
military account. Generous grants of citizenship round out
Rome's local conquests at the end of the first half; immediately she is challenged by the Samnites to fight for the
mastery of all Italy. Further, it is Rome's wise bestowal
of citizenship that actually enables her to assume an ex-
panded imperial role. The careful juxtaposition of the scenes
on citizenship and expansion at once organizes Rome's wars
into two distinct phases of conquest and underscores the wisdom of creating citizens out of the Latins. We will examine
later the broad approach to his material by which Livy
achieves this pointed contrast at mid-pentad.[2] Here we will
merely note a specific device which is important in creating

---

[1]The Second Samnite War dominates one and one-half
books of Livy, ending finally at IX.45.1-4.

[2]See below, 175-176.

this effect. Livy's treatment of the importance of citizenship in 338 is separated by over ten years from the outbreak
of hostilities with the Samnites in 327. Only by reiterating
the importance of extending citizenship in the case of
Privernum (in 329) does Livy achieve the close juxtaposition
of this issue with the next phase of conquest at the center
of Book VIII.[1]

As Rome enters an era of greater military power, Livy
also shows a decisive change in the approach to discipline.
In the early days of the city it was necessary to use severe
measures; now, however, gentler techniques are more effective.
Two scenes treat the issue: the imperium Manlianum (6.14-8.2)
and the quarrel of Fabius and Papirius (30.1-37.2). These
scenes show a Livy who is very aware of a gradual evolution
in the Roman character. The command of Manlius epitomizes
discipline in the old severe style; Livy shows his horror of
it, and portrays the grim impression it makes on Manlius'
army. In counterpoint to this scene, he portrays the quarrel
of Papirius and Fabius. There, he roundly approves the
adoption of more humane treatment of Rome's men-at-arms.

The events surrounding the imperium Manlianum are as
follows. Titus Manlius, son of the consul Titus Manlius
Torquatus, fights and defeats Geminus Maecius, a Tusculan
nobleman, in single combat; he thereby violates the consul's
edict (6.16) prohibiting any engagement with the enemy extra
ordinem. For this transgression his father orders his

---

[1]Note the brief treatment accorded the year 328 (22.1-4).

execution on the perfectly correct judgment that he has
flouted military discipline (7.15-17, 7.19).

Livy's treatment of the incident, however, emphasizes
only the severity of the punishment. For example, he never
assigns any moral stigma to young Manlius' actions.[1] Quite
the opposite: he engages Geminus with the intention of
vindicating Rome's honor. He will teach the Latins to have
no love of fighting Romans (7.6); the outcome of his single
combat will demonstrate which of the two peoples is superior
in war (7.7). Livy's sympathy for the young Manlius is evident in his description of the lad's proud return to camp;
he addresses his father with touching filial piety, little
knowing that in emulating his father he has earned his doom.
The effect is quite pathetic (7.13):[2] "'Vt me omnes' inquit,
 pater, tuo sanguine ortum uere ferrent, prouocatus equestria
haec spolia capta ex hoste caeso porto.'" We may also observe that Livy palliates Manlius' offense. Dionysius
apparently states[3] that the consuls prohibited fighting
extra ordinem in order to instill fear in the troops and curb
a virtual mutiny. In Livy, however, the urgency of the

---

[1]He is said merely to be forgetful of the consular edict
(7.8): "Oblitus itaque imperii patrii consulumque edicti,
praeceps ad id certamen agitur...". Manlius' youthful nature,
when goaded (7.4, 7.7), is induced to accept Maecius' challenge either by anger, or fate, or the shame of declining
(7.8). Even Torquatus calls his action specimen istud
uirtutis deceptum uana imagine decoris (7.18).

[2]The pathos is reinforced by foreshadowing of his doom
(7.8, 7.12).

[3]XV.4.5-6. Dionysius' full treatment of this event has
been lost, but references to it survive here and at VIII.79.2
in the Roman Antiquities.

command is much reduced: the consuls merely wish to avoid
confusion with an enemy so similar to the Romans (6.15-16).

The punishment meted out, by contrast, is portrayed as
harshly as possible; it represents the ancient seueritas
(6.14): "Agitatum etiam in consilio est ut, si quando unquam
seuero ullum imperio bellum administratum esset, tunc uti
disciplina militaris ad priscos redigeretur mores." Immediately after Manlius' return to camp, his father summons a
contio and formally pronounces his doom. The contrast
between the boy's piety at 7.13 and the cold, immediate
verdict of his father (7.15-19) heightens the severity of the
penalty. We may note that, in Dionysius' version, Torquatus
decorated his son with a crown for bravery before bringing
his accusation (VIII.79.2). Livy, in omitting this award,
heightens the immediacy, and hence the sternness, of the
punishment. The severity of the penalty is underscored elsewhere; it is an "atrocity" (8.1: atrocitas), "not only
horrible for the present, but a grim example for posterity"
(7.22: non in praesentia modo horrenda sed exempli etiam
tristis in posterum).[1] Most vivid is the reaction of the
soldiers to the punishment (7.20-22): astounded at its
harshness, all see the axes bared against themselves; after
the execution they spare neither tears nor curses as they
throng Manlius' funeral. Livy, who has already shown the

---

[1] At IV.29.6 Livy states that the fact that such commands
(imperia Manliana) take the Manlian name is an insignem
titulum crudelitatis. At VIII.12.4 he calls the command
truci.

achievement of _moderatio_ in leaders and _modestia_ in subordinates, observes with some horror that obedience such as this is based not on _modestia_, but on "terror" (7.20: _metu_).[1] He does concede at least that the punishment produced a salutary effect (8.1).

The quarrel of Lucius Papirius Cursor and Quintus Fabius Maximus Rullianus (30.1-37.2) further explores the concept of military discipline which has already been treated in the _imperium_ Manlianum. There, discipline was effective but cruel; is it necessary, then, to sacrifice humanity to achieve military strength? In this sequence, Livy shows that Rome learns the effectiveness of mingling _severitas_ with _comitas_. This more humane code of discipline, far from diminishing her military strength, actually increases it. The soldiers respond with enthusiasm to this treatment and, where they failed before, now defeat their enemies in decisive fashion.[2]

This sequence is of interest for another reason: it shows, with great clarity, certain traits of style which are peculiar to Livy. Close examination of the sequence reveals

---

[1] Livy reacts with similar horror to the punishment of Mettius Fufetius (I.28.11). Nor does he find shocking punishments altogether absent from later times; for example, the burial alive of Gauls and Greeks (XXII.57.6).

[2] This quarrel has also been analyzed by Erich Burck in Vom Menschenbild in der römischen Literatur, ed. E. Lefèvre (Heidelberg 1966) 344-348; Mary Ann S. Robbins, Heroes and Men in Livy 1-10 (Unpublished diss. Bryn Mawr 1968) 119 ff.; H. Taine, Essai sur Tite Live (Paris 1882) 255-271. None of these accounts, however, extends its analysis beyond 35.9; therefore they do not see the scene's overall significance for military discipline.

that the handling of characterization is particularly idiosyncratic. Papirius is not consistently portrayed in dealing
with his men; he appears now as extraordinarily severe, now
as a patriot seeking only what is just, then again as severe,
before finally learning a lesson of moderation in command.
In these phases he somersaults from antagonist to protagonist, and back once more to antagonist, emerging at the end
as a sympathetic figure once more. The problem with Fabius'
character is different. If it is a feature of literary
characterization that deeds characterize the doer, then there
ought to be no worse scoundrel on earth: such is the magnitude of his disobedience, and of his unrepentance. And yet
he is undeniably a sympathetic figure. It is useless, then,
to speak of literary characterization here. We shall see
that character is treated, not as an end in itself, but as a
means of expressing certain thematic lessons.[1]

The circumstances of the quarrel are as follows. After
the dictator Papirius has received doubtful auspices, he
sets forth to Rome to take them again. First, however, he
orders his _magister equitum_, Fabius, not to engage the foe in
his absence (30.2). Fabius, however, taking advantage of the
enemy's carelessness (30.3), attacks and wins a great victory
at Imbrinium (30.4-7). It is this victory, fought against
orders, which endangers military discipline and occasions
the quarrel between the two magistrates.

---

[1]Compare Livy's treatment of Valerius Publicola and
Quinctius; above, 59-64.

The sequence of events may be divided into four sections,
based on the various reversals in Papirius' character:
30.8-33.22, 33.23-35.9, 35.10-36.4, and 36.5-37.2.

In the first section, Papirius attempts to secure
Fabius' execution in order to restore military discipline.
His discipline is equated with that of Manlius Torquatus
(30.13);[1] he himself is portrayed as a man of savage, implacable anger as he pursues this discipline. Not only the
comments of others, but the narrative of the dictator's deeds
emphasize his wrath. When he hears of Fabius' victory, anger
is his emotion both in front of the senate (30.10) and as he
hastens back to camp (30.12). Fabius, learning of his approach, sounds the same theme as he appeals to the soldiers
for aid: he needs protection against "the dictator's cruelty,
against which there is no defense" (31.1: impotenti crudelitate
dictatoris). Papirius' fury is at the forefront of Fabius'
speech: iratum uirtuti alienae felicitatique (31.2); furere
quod se absente res publica egregie gesta esset (31.2); et
nunc id furere, id aegre pati (31.4). Fabius affirms that
Papirius' hostility threatens all ranks alike (31.6-7); his
conclusio rouses the army to defend their collective liberty by
flying to his aid (31.8-9). The army eagerly undertakes his
defense (32.1).

Papirius, immediately upon his arrival, summons an assembly and proceeds to question Fabius in oratio recta (32.1-8).

1"...dictatorem auidum poenae uenire, alternis paene
uerbis T. Manli factum laudantem." Cf. 34.2, 35.9.

There is severity in the very directness with which he presses
home his line of questioning.[1] Phrases such as itemque illud
interrogo (32.4) and simul illud (32.5) enhance the effect of
severity by giving the questions a structure which is formal,
direct, and terse.[2] His stern questions adhere unswervingly
to the issue of Fabius' guilt. Ought he to obey the dictator?
Ought he to observe the religious scruples which bind the
dictator? Did Papirius not forbid him to engage the enemy?
This line of questioning leads inevitably to his conclusion
that Fabius has violated military discipline (32.7).[3] He
commands the magister equitum to address himself only to
these questions, and bids the lictor stand ready to seize
him (32.8).

Fabius, unable to answer the dictator's questions without admitting his disobedience, perforce resorts to complaints
and accusations as he attempts to clear himself (32.9-10).
The dictator's wrath is "kindled anew" (32.10: redintegrata
ira) by this direct violation of his order to address only
specific questions; he orders the rods and axes readied to

---

[1]H. Taine, Essai sur Tite Live (Paris 1882) 261 speaks
of "ce terrible raisonnement," saying that the speech represents "la colère nourrie par la logique." He concludes, "Le
développement des preuves est le développement de la
passion."

[2]Note also the use of formal phrases with stern effect.
See 32.3: "quaero...de te Q. Fabi"; 32.3: "dicto audientem
esse"; 32.8: "Ad haec quae interrogatus es responde; at extra
ea caue uocem mittas. Accede, lictor."

[3]"quo tu imperio meo spreto, incertis auspiciis,
turbatis religionibus, aduersus morem militarem disciplinamque
maiorum et numen deorum ausus es cum hoste confligere."

administer punishment. The magister equitum, however, forestalls his intentions by breaking away from the lictors and
taking refuge among the soldiers (32.11).

The ensuing confrontation between the dictator and the
army again focuses on Papirius' anger. Although the soldiers
condemn his inclemency, his very gaze intimidates those who
stand near his tribunal (32.12-13). More importantly, several unidentified legati, standing about his chair, dispas-
sionately assess the situation for him (32.14-18). Their
judgment is to be accepted, by the conventions which Livy
follows,[1] as authoritative. Surprisingly, even though it
is Fabius who has committed the offense, it is Papirius
whom these legati take to task. They say that he must let
his anger cool (32.14) and not pursue the extreme penalty
(32.15). He is behaving as if "blinded with anger" (32.17:
occaecatus ira); his conduct belies his aetas and prudentia
(32.16) and harms the interests of the Republic (32.18).
Their efforts at restraining him, however, are counterpro-
ductive. Instead of reconciling him with his magister equitum,
they merely kindle his anger against themselves. They are

---

[1] Livy employs authoritative observers to point to the
"right" interpretation of events elsewhere. At IX.7.2-5
Calavius shows that the Romans' dejected looks after the
pax Caudina bode ill for the Samnites. At VIII.20.11
Plautius dismisses the complicity of the people of Privernum
in their town's defection. His judgment indicates the
authorized interpretation of events, even though it may not
withstand close scrutiny; see above, 108-109. We may note that
Livy also employs authoritative figures of a different kind:
people who point out correct courses of action, such as
Herennius Pontius (IX.3.4-13), Maharbal (XXII.51.1-4), and
Hannibal (XXXVI.7.1-21; see 15.2).

ordered from the tribunal, and the contio degenerates into a mob scene. In a fine touch, night ends the conflict as if on the battlefield (33.2).

Fabius is ordered to reappear on the following day. When informed that Papirius' wrath will blaze up anew (33.3),[1] however, he flees to Rome and the senate instead. The following scenes, before the senate and people, yet again stress the dictator's implacability: Papirius pursues him angrily (33.5: infensus), and their quarrel is renewed (33.5: iteratur deinde contentio). The dictator's obdurate determination to punish Fabius, even in spite of the senate's pleas, is repeatedly stressed.[2] Finally Marcus Fabius, father of the magister equitum, appeals to the majesty of the people to test whether Papirius, in his resolve, will overstep even the bounds respected by kings (33.8). When the people have gathered, the elder Fabius inveighs against Papirius' pride and cruelty (33.11: superbiam crudelitatemque): he is seeking a triumph over a Roman commander as if over some enemy leader (33.13). Most of all, Fabius contrasts examples of moderatio in dealing with all classes of society and the army with the conduct of Papirius (33.13): "quantum interesse inter moderationem antiquorum et nouam superbiam crudelitatemque!" At 33.14-17 Fabius shows exempla of moderation: Cincinnatus

---

[1]"...cum omnes adfirmarent infestius Papirium exarsurum, agitatum contentione ipsa exacerbatumque...".

[2]33.6: "Vbi cum deprecantibus primoribus patrum atque uniuerso senatu perstaret in incepto immitis animus..."; 33.7: "...apud te nec auctoritas senatus...ualet..."; 33.8: "...fugienti senatus iudicium...".

towards the consul Lucius Minucius;[1] Camillus towards Lucius
Furius, whom Camillus even chose later as his partner in
command;[2] and the people themselves who, though they held
all power, never imposed worse punishment than a fine even
upon incompetent commanders. It is notable that Fabius portrays each example as a rejection of ira: Cincinnatus non
ultra saeuisse (33.14); Camillus was moderatum irae (33.15);
and the people showed that ne iram quidem unquam atrociorem
fuisse...quam ut pecunia eos multaret (33.17). At 33.18-22
he demonstrates how unlike these exempla Papirius' actions
are. Against the plebeians' magnanimity towards defeated
commanders he contrasts the dictator's treatment of a victorious one (33.18).[3] Papirius' "anger and violence" (33.19:
iram uiolentiamque) are unbridled. Conduct such as his can
only spoil Rome's hour of victory and bring grief to her
defenders, comfort to her foes.

And yet Papirius is in the right. His magister equitum
did violate orders, flouting military discipline. Why, then,
does he fail to win the reader's sympathy? The answer seems
to stem largely from his speech before the army. There his
strict formality gives him the air of a bully. Beyond that,
he argues mostly on behalf of the formal rights of magisterial

---

[1]See III.26-29.

[2]See VI.22.25.

[3]"nunc ducibus populi Romani, quae ne uictis quidem
bello fas fuerit, uirgas et secures uictoribus et iustissimos
meritis triumphos intentari."

power.[1] He does not expand on the ill effects of Fabius'
example upon the soldiers--a topic potentially full of pathos
and moral issues. In emphasizing the topos _illegitimum_, he
fails to develop others: _inhonestum_, _intutum_, etc. Papirius
seems more concerned to enforce his own rights than to avert
possible harm to others. He could, then, have elicited
sympathy in his speech, but he lost the opportunity. His
speech demonstrates his own bad qualities, of which Fabius
complains, rather than the bad qualities of his opponent.
This unfavorable impression is reinforced not only by the
later references to his anger but by the actual description
of his deeds. Worst of all is his relentlessness in seeking
Fabius' execution. Unmoved, he rejects first the appeals of
the army, then those of the senate, and finally confronts
even the Roman people. It is this dogged pursuit of his
magister equitum,which in large measure makes him appear
implacable.

Livy's portrayal of Fabius shows that he treats the
magister equitum only as a foil, a device to magnify the
dictator's wrath. His treatment of Fabius particularly deserves examination because it shows clearly that he is
unconcerned with characterization as an end in itself. In the
magister equitum we have a man who joins battle with the
Samnites (30.4-7) in violation of explicit orders (30.2).
He breaks orders again at 32.9-11 when he speaks of matters
forbidden (32.8) by Papirius, and even hurls accusations at

---

[1]See, for example, 32.3.

the dictator. He then resists arrest by the lictors and flees
to the soldiers for protection--an act which nearly causes
sedition in the ranks (32.11-13). Finally, he even flees from
the camp to Rome, again flouting explicit orders (33.3).
Clearly, if Fabius were to be judged on the basis of his
actions, he would be rated a scoundrel of the worst sort. And
yet his evil deeds are never associated with an evil character.
Neither Livy nor any person in the narrative, save the irate
dictator, even cites them as offenses.[1] The reader actually
receives a very favorable impression of Fabius. The authoritative legati speak of him as an "extraordinary young man"
(32.15: unico iuueni) from a noble gens. Marcus Fabius can
even speak of his son's "personal merit and high birth"
(33.7: uirtus nobilitasque).

This remarkable gloss of Fabius' misdeeds brings out
Papirius' moral defects in two ways. First, by ignoring the
issue of Fabius' disobedience as he flies for aid to the
army and to Rome, Livy is able to focus on the dictator's
implacable anger. For it is precisely by relentlessly demanding the punishment of his magister equitum before the
army, the senate, and the people that Papirius shows his
implacability. Second, by portraying Fabius as an excellent
character instead of an evil one, Livy portrays the dictator's
anger in a most unfavorable light. Papirius' wrath would
destroy a fine and innocent man, not one who richly deserves
punishment.

---

[1]The legati attribute any possible offense by Fabius to
his youthfulness (32.15), not to his actual character. Cf. 30.4.

Although Livy disapproves of Papirius' discipline in the
Manlian mode, he nevertheless cannot ultimately condone
Fabius' disobedience either. Livy establishes this point by
using several remarkable literary devices in phase two of the
narrative (33.23-35.9).

Most striking is the complete reversal in the portrayal
of the dictator. Livy, to show that Fabius is wrong, now
"rehabilitates" Papirius. He suddenly suspends the dictator's
unfavorable characteristics and emphasizes for the first
time the positive strengths of his arguments. His anger, a
hallmark before, suddenly disappears; there is hardly a
reference to _ira_ in this entire section. So intent is Livy
to show Papirius favorably that, when he lists the principles
favoring either side (34.1-3), he even palliates the hated
imperium _Manlianum_. Elsewhere Livy calls it cruel butchery,
but here he sees it as "the common weal placed before the
love of a son" 34.2: _posthabita_ _filii_ _caritas_ _publicae_
utilitati). Seen in this aspect, Papirius' discipline is
even comparable to Lucius Brutus' much admired execution of
his own sons (34.3).[1]

Papirius delivers a speech (34.3-11) where he appears,
not as irate, but as a reasonable man demanding in Fabius'
punishment only what is just and necessary for the discipline
of the army (34.4).[2] Now, instead of emphasizing the

---

[1]See II.5.5-8.

[2]Burck in _Vom_ _Menschenbild_ _in_ _der_ _römischen_ _Literatur_,
ed. E. Lefèvre (Heidelberg 1966) 347 says of this speech,
"Hier ist in der Argumentation des Diktators jedes persönliche

prerogatives of a magistrate, he vividly stresses the evils
which attend the fall of discipline (34.7-8).[1] For the
destruction in this manner of Rome's armies, and her power,
it will be the defenders of Fabius' disobedience that must
accept the blame of posterity (34.11): "horum criminum uos
reos in omnia saecula offerte, tribuni plebi; uestra obnoxia
capita pro licentia Q. Fabi obicite."

His speech instantly resolves the quarrel. Fabius'
partisans, and even the Fabii themselves, seeing the consequences of undiscipline, admit his fault. Where before
they demanded that he not be punished, now they beg compas-
sion (35.2): "Tribuni quoque inclinatam rem in preces[2]
subsecuti orare dictatorem insistunt ut ueniam errori humano,
ueniam adulescentiae Q. Fabi daret; satis eum poenarum
dedisse." Their admission that disobedience is intolerable
wins for Fabius the pardon, but not the amnesty, of the

Ressentiment, jede Gemütswallung, jede Rechthaberei
verschwunden. Es geht allein um die Erhaltung der disciplina
rei militaris et rerum civilium als einem Grundpfeiler der
römischen Lebensordnung." Mary Ann S. Robbins, Heroes and
Men in Livy 1-10 (Unpublished diss. Bryn Mawr 1968) 138
acknowledges that "the dictator himself has learned to practice moderatio."

[1]"...non miles centurionis, non centurio tribuni, non
tribunus legati, non legatus consulis, non magister equitum
dictatoris pareat imperio, nemo hominum, nemo deorum
uerecundiam habeat, non edicta imperatorum, non auspicia
obseruentur...". The vividness derives from the sequence of
short statements and the several cases of anaphora. See
also 34.10.

[2]At 32.12 and 33.7 Livy said that the dictator's opponents resorted to preces. But in neither case did these
preces indicate an admission that the dictator was in the
right. In the former case they were backed by the threat of
sedition; in the latter, by the appeal to the people. Only

dictator (35.5-6). Most importantly, their admission removes the threat to military discipline (35.4):[1] "Tum dictator silentio facto 'bene habet' inquit, 'Quirites; uicit disciplina militaris, uicit imperii maiestas, quae in discrimine fuerunt an ulla post hanc diem essent.'"

A brief denouement (35.8-9) shows the restoration of harmony and emphasizes that military discipline was strengthened by the danger to Fabius every bit as much as it had been strengthened earlier by the execution of the young Manlius (35.9): "...firmatumque imperium militare haud minus periculo Q. Fabi quam supplicio miserabili adulescentis Manli uidebatur."

Livy has shown that Fabius' conduct was wrong. Why, then, has he emphasized the savagery of Papirius so greatly? The answer is to be found in the further evaluation of Papirius' conduct in phase three (35.10-36.4), where events demonstrate the destructive effects of harsh discipline.

No sooner has his quarrel with Fabius been composed than Papirius reverts to his old character. Livy refers to his "savage anger" (35.10: trucem...iram) and "grim edicts" (35.11: tristia edicta). Furthermore, he forbids his magister equitum to exercise his office in any way (36.1) in spite of their recent reconciliation. The effects of his reversion

---

now does the opposition yield unreservedly to Papirius, laying aside contentio (35.3).

[1]See also 35.7: "...populo Romano, cui uitam debes, nihil maius praestiteris quam si hic tibi dies satis documenti dederit ut bello ac pace pati legitima imperia possis."

to anger, however, are uniformly bad. It causes the needless
loss of a party of foragers (35.10-11) and alienates the
loyalties of the soldiers (35.12). With so little hold on
his men, he does not even frighten the enemy (36.2). Worst
of all, his severity costs him victory on the battlefield
(36.3-4):

> Ceterum tantum momenti in uno uiro L. Papirio
> fuit ut, si ducis consilia fauor subsecutus
> militum foret, debellari eo die cum Samnitibus
> potuisse pro haud dubio habitum sit; ita
> instruxit aciem [loco ac subsidiis], ita omni
> arte bellica firmauit; cessatum a milite ac
> de industria, ut obtrectaretur laudibus ducis,
> impedita uictoria est.

Papirius draws the proper lesson in section four
(36.5-37.2): it is his own conduct which obstructed victory.
Severity by itself commands fear, not respect; to be effective,
it must be mingled with kindliness (36.5): "Sensit peritus
dux quae res uictoriae obstaret: temperandum ingenium suum
esse et seueritatem miscendam comitati." Accordingly he
makes it his habit to visit the wounded, entrusting them by
name to the care of the legates, tribunes, and prefects
(36.6). His new popularity produces a complete change of
fortune on the battlefield; he crushes the Samnites so
thoroughly that they resolve never to engage him again
(36.8). As he ravages Samnium, Papirius further binds the
soldiers to himself by declaring that they may have all of the
booty taken in the campaign (36.9-10).[1] He forces the

---

[1]The omission of details concerning both the great
victory and the subsequent campaign is consistent with
Livy's focus on the dictator's character.

Samnites to sue for peace, then enters Rome in triumph
(36.11-37.1). Livy's ultimate compliment to the "new"
Papirius is that he says the Samnites, who received a
one-year truce, were again eager for war as soon as he left
office (37.2).

The achievement of Livy's narrative of this episode is
to show that Roman commanders have learned that a new,
kindlier form of military discipline is now more effective
than the severity of Manlius.[1] This episode also raises a
double challenge to conventional modes of interpreting Livy.
First, it refutes the blind assumption, frequently made in
Livian scholarship, that his text may be understood as a
portrayal of character.[2] We have already seen in the example

---

[1]Although ancient sources agree on the severity of
Papirius, only Livy develops this moral lesson. T. R. S.
Broughton, The Magistrates of the Roman Republic (New York
1951) Vol. I, 147 lists the relevant accounts: Inscr. Ital.
13.3.62--ILS 53; Val. Max. 2.7.8; 3.2.9; Frontin Str.
4.1.39; Dio fr. 36; Zon. 7.26; Eutrop. 2.8; Auct. Vir. Ill.
31 and 32; Degrassi 108, 414f. Dio cites the evil effects
of Papirius' anger upon the army. He emphasizes his wrath
far less than Livy, however, while portraying the dictator
far more sympathetically. In his version, Papirius actually
adopted an angry visage merely to "improve" his soldiers and
to gain added favor from the unexpectedness of the pardon.
Valerius Maximus and Frontinus both include the imperium
Manlianum and Papirius' treatment of Fabius in special
sections devoted to military discipline. Neither of them,
however, specifically links the two incidents; they are
merely unconnected cases within the same general category.

[2]Such is the case with Robbins, Heroes and Men in Livy
1-10 (Unpublished diss. Byrn Mawr 1968) 159, who concludes
that the aim of the quarrel was to "round out the character
of this man [sc. Papirius] and to give realistic complexity
to his personality." Even Erich Burck in Vom Menschenbild
in der römischen Literatur, ed. E. Lefèvre (Heidelberg 1966)
345 falls into this trap. Dealing with Fabius' oration
rousing the troops to his defense (31.1-9), Burck speaks as
if Livy were engaged in characterization: "Er [sc. Fabius]

of Valerius Corvus that character might be drawn only when
it suited Livy's larger historical purpose. In this episode
it is hardly possible to speak of characterization at all.
Fabius is regarded as a good man in spite of his flagrantly
bad deeds. Papirius, alternating between severity and moderation, plays the antagonist in phases one and three of the
narrative, the protagonist in phases two and four. In this
episode, therefore, even the nature of character is deter-
mined by the external requirements of the narrative, not the
inner qualities of individuals.[1] Second, our examination of
VIII.30.1-37.2 suggests that the proper evaluation of the

---

setzt sich dadurch erneut ins Unrecht, obwohl er doch
vielmehr die Möglichkeit einer Entschuldigung beim Diktator,
einer sachlichen Erklärung seiner Beweggründe oder einer
Vermittlungsaktion durch seine Offiziere hätte ins Auge
fassen müssen." Such an analysis might be germane to most
authors, but it does nothing to shed light on Livy's aims.
Livy must be treated by his own particular aesthetic standards.

[1] In the Third Decade it is possible to speak of the
characterization of, for example, Quintus Fabius Maximus
Cunctator. He is given a distinct and consistent (albeit
hardly complex) personality which then affects the course of
events; that is, it is he and no other, who advises Paullus
against engaging Hannibal (XXII.39) and who opposes Scipio's
invasion of Africa (XXVIII.40-42). It is quite the opposite
with Papirius and at least most of the other heroes in the
First Decade. The rapidity of Livy's treatment of these
years, and the paucity of source material, leave little
scope for drawing well-developed characters. To be sure,
certain virtues do emerge from their conduct before the
senate, in battle, in their dealings with defeated enemies,
etc. It cannot be said of them, however, that their
characters mold external events; rather it is the record of
events which defines their characters. Demonstrating, in
various adventures, now fides, now moderatio, now comitas,
they become agglomerates of whatever virtues (or vices)
attach to the deeds which history has associated with their
names. They acquire no internal consistency; hence nobody
feels the slightest surprise when Manlius Capitolinus, a
hero in Book V, turns seditious in Book VI.

episode requires the reader to accept certain superficial impressions which Livy has studiously created, even though reflection shows them false.[1] In this case it must be accepted that Fabius is a fine man in spite of his bad deeds, so that Papirius' wrath might seem excessive.[2]

The literary effect of the Ab Urbe Condita, then, depends on its own internal laws. Modes of interpretation which work elsewhere may fail to illuminate the text of Livy. The critic must accordingly beware of judging Livy by these methods.

The thematic unity of these two pairs of scenes, and their structural balance, formally unify Book VIII around a central motif: the sources of Rome's military strength.[3]

---

[1]The principle is well illustrated at VI.22.6-24.11, where Camillus is clearly intended to be perceived as prudent and correct in declining battle with the Volsci. His colleague, Lucius Furius Medullinus, is clearly rash; he offers battle, and is on the point of being routed when Camillus' intervention turns defeat into victory. Camillus' superiority is emphasized from the start (22.6): "Volscum bellum M. Furio extra ordinem decretum; adiutor ex tribunis sorte L. Furius datur, non tam e re publica quam ut collegae materia ad omnem laudem esset...quod rem temeritate eius prolapsam restituit...". Yet further reflection would show that in fact Medullinus was right to engage the enemy that day. Once all the troops were involved, they achieved victory. There is no point in Camillus' desire to postpone battle; it is in fact he, not Medullinus, whose strategic judgment is wrong. The reader does not notice this, however; nor is he meant to. Here, as at VIII.30.1-37.2, the reader must accept certain superficial impressions, studiously created by Livy, in evaluating the scene. See above, 26-27, 92-94.

[2]Perhaps Livy could have avoided the problems of characterization here by depicting both Fabius and Papirius from the start as partly right, partly wrong: a morally gray situation. In so doing, however, it seems to this writer that he would have lost the exciting story of men in conflict.

[3]Only one substantial scene in Book VIII contradicts the general portrait of Rome's moral excellence: the trial and

Livy thereby creates, as a centerpiece for the pentad, a
strong thematic statement of the reasons for Rome's growth in
Books VI-X.

The dramatic tempo of the book complements its thematic
focus; it portrays the growing ascendancy of Rome's power.
Rome's position is clearly jeopardized by the Latin Rebellion
at the beginning of the book; her weakness is attested before
the revolt (2.12). At 4.7-10 the Latin Annius comments on
Rome's failure to punish the Latins' independent actions as
a sign of her weakness.[1] Yet the note of Roman weakness does
not last long. The Latins' boldness soon appears as folly;
at 5.2 Annius cuts a ridiculous figure as he addresses the
Senate "as if he had captured the Capitoline by force of
arms, and were not speaking as an ambassador protected by the
law of nations."[2] The consul Manlius condemns Annius' demands for the Latins' equality with scorn and vigor (5.7-10);
Rome has recovered her ascendancy by 6.1-7, where Annius'
fall down the steps foreshadows Rome's victory. Thereafter
Livy does not cite Roman weakness; the Latins variously appear, in scattered references, sometimes as formidably like
the Romans, sometimes as an easy conquest for Roman arms.

---

conviction of Roman matrons on charges of poisoning at
18.1-13. Perhaps Livy's concern for the portrait of Rome's
moral excellence, augmenting his natural horror at the
matrons' deeds, explains his exceptional expression of regret
about the facts of the case (18.2).

[1]See also 3.1 and 5.4.

[2]"...tamquam uictor armis Capitolium cepisset, non
legatus iure gentium tutus loqueretur...".

These conflicting allusions to them now as formidable, now as
weak, can occur virtually side by side.[1] The explanation for
their portrayal in this fashion seems to be that Livy has
two divergent objects in mind: to prepare the reader to accept their admission as Roman citizens,[2] and yet to show
that Rome will win the war.[3]

Rome of course defeats the Latins severely. Manlius
wins his single combat at 7.1-12, while Decius' devotio
dramatically highlights a major victory at Veseris
(8.19-10.10). Yet it is the battle at 11.5-16 which first
shows the Latin cause desperate. At 11.6-8 the Latin commander, Numisius, strains credibility in attempting to claim
equal share of victory in the earlier battle of Veseris.
Livy shows his contempt for such an interpretation at 11.10
where Numisius' written claims are called "deceitful letters"

---

[1]The Latins are portrayed as formidably similar to the
Romans themselves at 4.3, 6.14-15, 8.2, and 8.14-18. We
have seen that at 5.2 Livy casts ridicule on Annius' bold
speech of 5.3-6; Annius' fall at 6.1-7 reinforces the effect.
The Latins' weakness is of course also evident in their
defeats, which are treated below.

[2]Similarity to the Romans is cited as a cause for
citizenship only at 21.8-10, where the men of the Volscian
town of Privernum love liberty in the true Roman fashion.
Yet the general similarity of the Latins and Romans, stressed
early in Book VIII, must be regarded as preparation for their
receiving citizenship. See VII.24.4, where the consul
Popilius exclaims that Rome can make citizens out of Latins
and Sabines, but not Gauls.

[3]The technique resembles that which we have already
observed in the quarrel of Papirius and Fabius. There, his
pursuit of divergent aims--to condemn Papirius' anger as
excessive, and yet to acknowledge that his authority was
intolerably flouted--caused him to portray the dictator
variously as an unsympathetic and as a sympathetic figure.
Above, 115-130.

which appeal to "those who, not being present at the battle,
were the more willing to put blind faith" in his claims.[1]
The Latins then gather a _tumultuarius_ _exercitus_ to face the
Roman regulars; we are well prepared to expect their swift
defeat at Trifanum and the surrender of Latium and Campania
(11.11-12); terms of surrender are then described at
11.13-16. This battle, though briefly described, emphasizes
afresh Rome's decisive military superiority.

Hostilities are renewed the following year (339); in
spite of some successes there is little decisive effect
achieved by the consuls at 12.5-9. The tempo of Roman expansion picks up again, however, in 338 (13.1-9). The Latins
are said to be in desperate straits at the year's outset
(13.2); a series of Roman victories (13.4-7) reduces them to
final submission (13.8-9). The stage is set for the debates
on the grants of citizenship which, as we have seen, will
establish Roman power on an enduring basis.

Although there are no important battles between the
Latin and the Samnite wars, several signs indicate that the
beginning of hostilities with Samnium marks a far greater
expansion of Roman power. The importance of the war, and of
the challenge to fight for peninsular supremacy, are marked
by a great deal of foreshadowing: 17.3, 17.8, 19.3, 20.12,
22.7, 22.9-10 and 23.1.

---

[1]"Fallacibus litteris circa Latium nomenque Volscum
missis, quia qui non interfuerant pugnae ad credendum temere
faciliores erant, tumultuarius undique exercitus raptim
conscriptus conuenit."

Events go well for Rome virtually from the start of the
new conflict. Livy briefly notes that the Lucani and Apuli
enter into friendship with the Romans (25.3); meanwhile, the
Romans capture three Samnite towns (25.4).[1] At 25.5 he
foreshadows Rome's success in the war against Naples. Livy
recounts the capture of the town in detail (25.5-26.7); the
Samnites even look ridiculous as they flee home unarmed
(26.4-5). Yet the impact of these events in aiding Rome's
expansion is not fully felt until 27.1-5, where as we saw
above[2] the Tarentines, seeing Rome's new alliance with the
Apuli and Lucani and her conquest of Naples, realize that she
is alarmingly close to peninsular domination (27.3-4). A
relative lull follows during the quarrel of Papirius and
Fabius; the victory of Fabius at 30.4-7 serves rather to
inflame the dictator than to endanger the Samnite cause. At
36.8-12, however, Papirius defeats them so thoroughly that
they decline to engage him again, allowing instead the unre-
strained plunder of their lands; they finally sue for peace.[3]
Their desperate situation is apparent at 37.5, where they
are "barely able at that time to keep the war at arm's length
from themselves."[4]

---

[1]Livy notes these as propitious beginnings of the war
(25.5): "Hoc bello tam prospere commisso...".

[2]See above, 110-111.

[3]They obtain a one-year's truce at 37.2, but break it at
37.3.

[4]"...Samnitium, uix a se ipsis eo tempore propulsantium
bellum...". The Samnites' conspicuous ill-fortune in these
times is referred to also at 38.10: "...iam pridem desueto
Samnite clamorem Romani exercitus pati...".

It remains for the final battle of the book (38.1-39.9), however, to culminate the military ascendancy which has been growing through the book. The length of this battle in the narrative, the bitterness with which it is fought, and the decisiveness of the outcome--plus its position at the end of the book--all contribute to this scene's forcefulness as the climax of Book VIII. In Livy the most crushing military defeats are often administered after the most prolonged and bitter struggle.[1] So here the Samnites prosper initially; they surprise the Romans by attacking their camp (38.2) and harass them as they withdraw from the camp (38.5-6). The ensuing battle is prolonged and bitter: from the third hour until the eighth, the issue is so fiercely contested that there is neither advance nor retreat, nor the slightest respite for either side (38.10-11). Finally the Samnite cavalry, seeing the Roman baggage undefended, plunder it (38.12). Their act loses the battle, however; the Romans attack them while encumbered with booty and nearly annihilate them (38.13-39.3). The Roman horse then envelops the Samnite line from either wing (39.3) and the Samnite infantry is at last defeated decisively. Those who stand and fight are surrounded and slaughtered; others, taking to their heels, are massacred by the cavalry (39.8-9). Among those slain is

---

[1] Cf. II.19.3-20.13, VII.33.5-18, IX.39.5-11, etc. At IX.40.1-17 and X.38.1-42.7 we have a similar device: Roman victories are made to seem the more decisive not by the enemy's stubborn resistance in battle but by the elaborate descriptions of enemy preparations.

their commander.[1]

The consequences of this battle are fully described by
Livy: the Samnites, their power broken, are moved to seek
peace and to make amends for a war impiously waged in violation of a treaty (39.10-11):

> Hoc demum proelium Samnitium res ita infregit,
> ut omnibus conciliis fremerent minime id
> quidem mirum esse, si impio bello et contra
> foedus suscepto, infestioribus merito deis
> quam hominibus nihil prospere agerent:
> expiandum id bellum magna mercede luendumque
> esse....

They resolve to turn over to the Romans those guilty of the
war,[2] all the Roman booty and captives, and whatsoever the
fetiales demand. When Brutulus Papius, on whom alone the
war-guilt rests, commits suicide, his body and possessions
are offered (39.12-14). The Romans, however, reject the
Samnites' overture for peace, accepting only the captives and
whatever booty can be recognized (39.15). The Samnites'
power to resist seems broken permanently.[3] This result
stands as a fitting climax to the book's overall tempo; it is

---

[1]Livy prefers this version of events over another one
according to which the consuls, not Cornelius, defeated the
Samnites (40.1). Whether this variant differed substantially
from Livy's account of the battle itself cannot be known;
perhaps it did not, as Livy often indicates such differences.

[2]See 39.11: "...id referre tantum utrum supplicia noxio
paucorum an omnium innoxio praebeant sanguine...". As at
20.11, guilt is deftly removed by imputing it not to the
people at large but only to specific auctores armorum; see
above, 108-109.

[3]See Burck in Vom Menschenbild in der römischen
Literatur, ed. E. Lefèvre (Heidelberg 1966) 325: "Der
Widerstand der Samniten scheint gebrochen. Roms Endsieg
nicht ferne zu sein."

the logical outcome of the Romans' growing power.

Book VIII therefore achieves a unified dramatic effect
as follows. The Latin War represents for Rome essentially
a process of consolidation and recovery from the weakness
explicit at the book's start. The Second Samnite War represents a new and important expansion of Roman power: her
ambitions now extend over the entire peninsula. The tempo
of victory is much greater in the Samnite conflict: the narrative of the war itself occupies a greater part of the book,
and is more emphatically introduced; most importantly, it
leads into a particularly striking note of success at the
book's end where a decisive victory apparently smashes Samnite resistance. Length, the description of the stakes
involved, and the resolution of events all show that the
Second Samnite War is far more important even than the Latin
War. The book achieves a unified effect: from weakness,
Rome consolidates, then expands to previously unattained
power.

Despite Rome's virtually unbroken military successes in
Book VIII, several comments introduce a discordant note into
the narrative. The prospect of war with the Vestini (29.1-5)
seems, albeit briefly, to challenge the very security of
Rome itself.[1] Likewise the mere rumor of a Gallic attack
causes the appointment of a dictator and the levy of a large
army at 17.6-7; at 20.2-5 the Roman fear of a Gallic attack

---

[1]See 29.1. The suspense ends quickly at 29.5: "sed
euentus docuit fortes fortunam iuuare;" the Vestini are soon
routed decisively (29.11-14).

is more thoroughly developed. These details, which contrast
with the pattern of Roman success, give rise to a dramatic
tension[1] even though the ultimate outcome of events is well
known.[2]

The thematic integrity of the book is maintained by one
literary device whose importance must not be underrated.
Livy is fond, at the ends of his books, of foreshadowing
prosperity or disaster in the next book.[3] Here at the close
of Book VIII, however, there is not the slightest hint of the
disaster at the Caudine Forks which immediately begins
Book IX.[4] The failure to foreshadow is made all the more
remarkable by the fact that circumstances would seem to call
for the device; it is the very refusal to accept the Samnites'
expiation described at 39.10-15 which will make the Romans
morally responsible for the Caudine disaster.[5] That Livy
eschews the device of foreshadowing here is explicable in

---

[1]The foreshadowing of the major wars with the Latins
and Samnites also creates dramatic tension, without
necessarily boding ill for Rome; see 2.12, 3.1, 3.8, 17.2,
17.8, 19.3, 20.12, 22.7, 22.9-10, 23.1, etc.

[2]Compare Burck's comments on the psychology of Books
XXVI, XXI and XXII, in Livy, ed. T. A. Dorey (London and
Toronto 1971) 25-26.

[3]The ends of Books XXI and XXII provide the most famous,
as well as most effective, examples of the technique.
Flaminius' failure to observe proper ritual in entering the
consulship (XXI.63.13-14) foreshadows the defeats of Book
XXII. The stirring reception given the consul Varro after
Cannae (XXII.61.14-15), however, shows Rome's spirit unbroken and portends her recovery in the coming books.

[4]See IX.1.1: "Sequitur hunc annum nobilis clade Romana
Caudina pax T. Veturio Caluino Sp. Postumio consulibus."

[5]See IX.1.3-11.

only one fashion. Book VIII centers thematically on the
sources of Rome's military excellence and, in line with that
excellence, portrays the unbroken growth of Roman power
through the book. To foreshadow great disaster at its end,
therefore, would be to spoil the book's effect. The irony of
coming disaster would mock the power of Roman arms just in
their hour of greatest triumph. The thematic integrity of
the book therefore demands that he not foreshadow the Caudine
defeat.

In closing, we should note that apart from the major
incidents illustrating the sources of Rome's military power
through the narrative, there are an unusual number of fine
illustrations in Book VIII of Rome's military excellence.
Outstanding among these is the single combat of Titus
Manlius (7.1-12) which, aside from demonstrating the harshness of early discipline, shows also the superiority of the
Roman over the Latin knight.[1] The devotio of P. Decius Mus
(9.1-12) likewise exemplifies Roman heroism in striking
fashion, and helps Rome to win a major victory over the
Latins (8.19-10.10). Courageous deeds, like that of Decius,
contribute nothing to Livy's specific explanation of why
Rome's military power grows at this point. Romans, after
all, have performed brave deeds before and will continue to
perform them. Yet the great feats of valor surely do adorn

---

[1]Maecius' challenge at 7.7 establishes the combat as a
programmatic test of Latin versus Roman skill: "Visne igitur
...tu ipse congredi mecum, ut nostro duorum iam hinc euentu
cernatur quantum eques Latinus Romano praestet?" Cf. VII.9.8.

the annals of the Roman military. And they are a general
reminder that the fortunes of Rome depend ultimately on the
excellence of her people.[1]

BOOK IX

The Samnite challenge to determine Italian hegemony, and
the onset of the Second Samnite War, set in motion a tempo of
Roman success which extends, virtually unbroken, through the
remainder of the pentad's second half. While Books IX and X
may each, of themselves, create a strong impression of Rome's
march to victory,[2] they are only a part--historically and
dramatically--of the larger movement towards Italian hegemony

---

[1]Still other incidents, which perhaps deal implicitly
with Roman military excellence or the expansion of Roman
power, can scarcely be said to contribute to the dramatic
progress or thematic content of the book. Such incidents
are generally the bare facts inevitable in Livy's early
annalistic history; while they may be expected generally
to conform with the large historical trends which he has
developed, they do little to help formulate those trends
dramatically. At 37.8-12 the Tusculans are not punished for
their role in stirring Velitrae and Privernum to make war
against Rome. Yet Livy makes no comment on Rome's moderate
policies, as he did at VIII.13-14 and 21; indeed, he emphasizes the harsh <u>sententia</u> of the Pollian tribe against the
Tusculans rather than the mildness of the other tribes.
Similar are the brief accounts of battles won (16.1-3,
16.6-11, 17.1, 29.11-14, etc.), colonies sent out (14.7,
14.8, 16.13-14, 21.11, and 22.1-2), or new tribes established
(17.11). These events are simply the mechanical facts of
history, recorded without elaboration. While they do not
give shape to Livy's major theme, they do flesh it out. Without small scenes like these, the great scenes would give no
impression of epitomizing the historical developments of an
era.

[2]Book IX shows an internal "movement" towards greater
Roman strength: it chronicles the revenge exacted for the
humiliation of Caudium, and the Samnites' surrender. Book X
covers events from the outbreak of the Third Samnite War until
the apparent destruction of the enemy's power to resist.

which begins with the Samnites' challenge at VIII.23.

There is, to be sure, variation in the pace of the
narrative. Several times Livy hints darkly of difficult
battles to come, or of Roman power threatened. These threats
add dramatic interest to the pace of the narrative, but do
not alter Rome's overall progress to virtual peninsular
hegemony. Actual events which would contradict Rome's
growing power, however, are rigorously subordinated to the
main progress of the narrative. For example, Livy must
inevitably record a certain number of minor setbacks. His
perfunctory treatment of them reflects their unimportance;
they do not impede Rome's progress to power. Even when a
major defeat is incurred at Caudium, Livy treats it in such
a fashion as to minimize its effect.

As we have already seen, Book IX begins with the Roman
disaster at Caudium. Yet just as Livy's desire to emphasize
Roman strength in Book VIII caused him not to foreshadow
Caudium, so now his desire to show Rome's progress to
peninsular hegemony molds in remarkable fashion his account
of the battle and its aftermath.

Heinz Bruckmann's account of Roman defeats may be con-
sulted for the similarities between the Caudine disaster and
other Roman defeats.[1] Yet the most striking thing about
Caudium is that--unlike the defeats of Books XXI and XXII,
which are intended to begin the third decade on a bleak though

---

[1]Heinz Bruckmann, Die römischen Niederlagen im
Geschichtswerk des T. Livius (diss. Munster 1936) 3-31.

dramatic note--Livy endeavors mightily to minimize its significance.[1] Livy achieves this effect by attributing the
setback to temporary factors: terrain; a sudden and inexplicable loss of character, along with bad generalship; and most
importantly, the loss of divine favor. Livy emphasizes the
transience of these factors; the account of Caudium abundantly
foreshadows the Romans' recovery of their usual character,
their return to divine favor, and their resounding victories
over the Samnites. The main interest in Livy's account,
therefore, lies not in the defeat but in the process by which
the defeat is annulled and reversed, with emphasis on the
great victories to come.

Livy emphasizes that the defeat occurs under special
circumstances: terrain is a decisive factor. The Romans are
caught in an open area, girt by unbroken mountains and
accessible only through narrow passes on either end (2.6-8).
Topography must of course figure largely in any discussion of
Caudium. But here its effect surpasses all credibility. The
Romans are surrounded without even making contact with the
enemy, much less suffering a defeat at their hands.[2] Nor can
the trapped Romans come to grips with the foe at all (3.3):
"quo aut qua eamus? num montes moliri sede sua paramus? dum
haec imminebunt iuga, qua tu ad hostem uenies?"[3] Although

----

[1]He played down the defeat at the Allia in similar
fashion at V.38.1-10; see Luce, TAPhA 102 (1971) 278-279.

[2]They do no more than see the enemy (2.9-10) and hear
their insults (2.14). Later, Livy mentions several unsuccessful attempts to break out (4.1).

[3]See also 4.9.

Livy acknowledges the Romans' temporary loss of character here, he uses topography to spare them the blame of an outright defeat. Since he will shortly emphasize the army's ability to humble the Samnites, he is pleased to attribute the Caudine defeat to circumstances, not the foe.

Beyond the difficulties of terrain, the Roman defeat is incurred largely through an inexplicable aberration of character.[1]

> Immediately upon falling into the Samnites' trap the whole army simply comes to a halt; no orders whatsoever are issued. The soldiers, gripped by an unaccustomed sluggishness (torpor...insolitus), stare about as if their neighbors might be more in possession of their faculties (compotem magis mentis ac consilii) (2.10-11).

> They finally begin to entrench their position, at no one's command and without any soldierly exhortation, pathetically ridiculing as they work the futility of their labors (2.12-14).

> The consuls in their dejection fail even to call their legates and tribunes, who convene unbidden at their headquarters (2.15).

> At nightfall the army is still lamenting, not planning. While some wish for a chance to engage the enemy on any terrain, others despairingly respond that their position has doomed them: armed and unarmed, brave and coward, all have been captured and beaten (3.1-3).

The Romans' loss of identity could scarcely be more pointed.

The consuls' failure to issue orders after the trap has been sprung seems merely a part of the general torpor gripping

---

[1]Luce, TAPhA 102 (1971) 269-271 finds that a similar aberration of character was responsible for the Gallic capture of Rome in Book V.

the whole army at 2.10-3.3.[1] Their poor generalship, however,
is blamed at 5.6-7 as a major factor causing the disaster in
the first place (5.7): "...illis non ducem locorum, non
exploratorem fuisse; beluarum modo caecos in foueam missos."[2]

Most importantly, the Romans' defeat at Caudium springs
from their loss of divine favor. They alienated the gods by
refusing the Samnites' application for a just peace
(VIII.39.10-15); the lesson is explicitly drawn by Caius
Herennius Pontius' address to the Samnites at 1.3-11 (1.11):
"pro certo habete priora bella aduersus deos magis quam
homines gessisse, hoc quod instat ducibus ipsis dis gesturos."

It is one of Livy's compliments to the Romans that their
defeats never stem from a permanent flaw of character, as
other peoples' often do.[3] This single fact guarantees the
Romans' ascendancy, for divine anger, deviations from normal

---

[1]Similarly the consuls' refusal to transact public
business after their return to Rome (7.12) is symptomatic of
the whole army's desire for revenge. We may note that the
consuls' failure to issue orders at 2.10-3.3 is the result
of dramatic necessity: if the army is to be portrayed as
listless and purposeless, the consuls must be providing no
direction.

[2]The Samnites' fraus which fooled the consuls is
described at 2.1-4.

[3]For example, Livy characterizes the Volsci as a
"ferocior ad rebellandum quam ad bellandum gens" (VII.27.7);
the Greeks are a "gente lingua magis strenua quam factis"
(VIII.22.8). The Tarentines emerge, in Papirius Cursor's
estimation, as a "uanissimam...gentem," unable even to
master their own affairs (IX.14.5). Of the Gauls Livy says:
"longiore certamine...Gallorum quidem etiam corpora intol-
erantissima laboris atque aestus fluere, primaque eorum
proelia plus quam uirorum, postrema minus quam feminarum
esse" (X.28.4). See also the programmatic characterization
of the Gaul at VII.9.6-10.14; above, 95.

character, and bad generalship all cause only temporary
setbacks. The Romans' strength is abiding because it is
founded in their abiding character;[1] this character is the
source and cause of Rome's military success throughout the
extant books of the _Ab Urbe Condita_.[2]

Although the Romans must surrender their army upon the
Samnites' terms (4.1-5), Livy stresses the temporariness of
the defeat. In the very moment of their triumph the Samnites
seem fatally blinded by the gods.[3] Not knowing what terms to
impose upon the Romans (3.4), they turn for advice to old
Herennius Pontius (3.4-13). He, a Teiresias figure,[4] wisely
advises them to kill or befriend the Romans, but not to
humiliate them; humiliation will stir them to exact several-
fold revenge. Despite his counsel the Romans are sent under

---

[1]See Calavius' opinion of the battle (7.3-5), which is
quoted below, 147 n.1. The importance of national
character is implicit also in the verdict, albeit a mistaken
verdict, of the young Capuan nobles upon the battle (6.12-13):
"...iacere indolem illam Romanam ablatosque cum armis animos
...habere Samnites uictoriam non praeclaram solum sed etiam
perpetuam; cepisse enim eos non Romam, sicut ante Gallos,
sed, quod multo bellicosius fuerit, Romanam uirtutem
ferociamque...".

[2]See Preface 9: "ad illa mihi pro se quisque acriter
intendat animum, quae uita, qui mores fuerint, per quos uiros
quibusque artibus domi militiaeque et partum et auctum
imperium sit...". Since success in war stems from national
character, Livy must praise at least some aspects of the
character of Rome's more formidable enemies, such as the
Samnites (VII.33.16, X.31.11-14). The Ligurians are called
a _durum in armis genus_ at XXVII.48.10; see also XXXIX.1. He
also singles out certain of the Macedonians for praise
(XLV.30.7).

[3]Compare Hannibal, who is similarly stricken by the
hands of the gods after Cannae (XXII.51.3-4).

[4]For authoritative figures who point out the correct
course of action, see above, 119 n.1.

the yoke. The enormity of this foolish deed is apparent at
4.10-16, for by sparing the Roman army it is clear that the
Samnites have lost their chance to destroy Rome.[1] Again at
7.1-5 Livy shows that the Samnites' very success will redound
to their sorrow. Finally, Postumius states outright that
the gods have beguiled the Samnites out of their triumph
(9.10-12).[2]

Along with these indications that Rome will recover,
Livy devotes most of his account to tracing in detail the
restoration of conditions which will allow Rome to efface
the defeat. Three things are needed: Romans must regain
their own character; they must free themselves from the terms
of the Caudine peace; and they must regain the favor of the
gods which they forfeited at VIII.39.10-15.

The very humiliation inflicted on the Romans brings
them back to their own proper character. Livy emphasizes the
depth of their emotions as they undergo the ignominy of
surrender.

> They groan, as if condemned to death, upon hearing
> the terms of peace (4.6).

> They reflect bitterly on each stage of the coming
> humiliation: the surrender of weapons; the passage
> under the yoke; the wretched march through allied
> territory; the return in defeat, not the accustomed
> triumph, to Rome: unwounded, unarmed, untested in
> battle, they are beaten (5.8-10).

> The actual humiliation of the yoke, "more bitter
> to experience than they had imagined" (5.11: ...

---

[1]The patriotic motives behind the Roman's surrender here
even exempt these armies from moral censure.

[2]See also 9.14-15.

omnia tristiora experiundo...quam quae praeceperant
animis.), is described in detail: the passage, unarmed, beyond the rampart; the surrender of hostages;
the humiliation of the consuls; the actual passage
under the yoke, jeered and mistreated by the enemy
(5.11-6.2).

The march towards Capua is made hateful by the very
light of day. The soldiers, stung by shame, elect
to spend the night in the open rather than in the
city; when met by the Capuans, they steadfastly avoid
even their gaze (6.3-9).

Having arrived back in Rome, the soldiers shut
themselves in their houses for several days; the
consuls also, hidden from sight, carry on no public
business except to name a dictator comitiorum causa
at the senate's express wish (7.10-12).

At 6.10-13 certain Capuan nobles interpret the Romans'
conduct as a sign that their spirit has been broken. They
are refuted by Aulus Calavius, who interprets the humiliation
properly: the Romans' silence and the shame will soon exact
bitter retribution upon the Samnites.[1] In this fashion the
entire account of the Romans' humiliation is made ironic.
Far from adorning the Samnites' victory, it powerfully indicates the restoration of the Romans' character and the doom
which overhangs their foe.

Livy also establishes an important technical point:
Rome is not bound by the Caudine peace, and may justly renew
the war. At 5.1-6 he emphatically states that peace was

---

[1] 7.3-5: "silentium illud obstinatum fixosque in terram
oculos et surdas ad omnia solacia aures et pudorem intuendae
lucis ingentem molem irarum ex alto animo cientis indicia esse;
aut Romana se ignorare ingenia aut silentium illud Samnitibus
flebiles breui clamores gemitusque excitaturum, Caudinaeque
pacis aliquanto Samnitibus quam Romanis tristiorem memoriam
fore; quippe suos quemque eorum animos habiturum, ubicumque
congressuri sint; saltus Caudinos non ubique Samnitibus
fore.

arranged by a _sponsio_, not a _foedus_. At 8.3-10 Postumius
points out that this legal distinction allows Rome to
repudiate the settlement; if the _sponsores_ are bound over to
the Samnites the war may be justly renewed.[1] Two obvious
objections are raised against Postumius' proposal to surrender
the _sponsores_ (8.14-15): first, that the Romans, in repudiat-
ing the settlement, must restore to the Samnites every advantage which they gave up by agreeing to the peace; second,
that the plebeian tribunes cannot be surrendered since they
are sacrosanct. The first objection is refuted at length by
Postumius, on the grounds that the _sponsio_ was never approved
by the Roman people (9.1-19). The second is circumvented by
the voluntary abdication of the tribunes, that they might be
bound over with the rest (10.1-2).

Rome's moral recovery, and her legal ability to seek
vengeance upon the Samnites, then, are established in detail
with powerful foreshadowing of the Samnites' doom. Livy
states that "a new dawn seemed to arise upon the state"[2]
when the Romans realized they were not bound by the peace;
the desire to avenge the defeat burned strong.[3]

The final stage of the Roman recovery begins at 10.10

---

[1]See 8.6: "Dedamur per fetiales nudi uinctique;
exsoluamus religione populum, si qua obligauimus, ne quid
diuini humaniue obstet quo minus iustum piumque de integro
ineatur bellum."

[2]10.2: "...lux quaedam adfulsisse ciuitati uisa est."

[3]10.5: "Arma cuncti spectant et bellum: en unquam
futurum, ut congredi armatis cum Samnite liceat?" At 10.6
the state is said to burn "ira odioque".

where Postumius, bound over to the Samnites and technically

therefore a Samnite citizen, kicks the Roman fetial in the

knee. This violation of the ius gentium supersedes the

Romans' offence at VIII.39.10-15 and restores their claim to

divine favor: "Haec dicenti fetiali Postumius genu femur

quanta maxime poterat ui perculit et clara uoce ait se

Samnitem ciuem esse, illum legatum [fetialem] a se contra ius

gentium uiolatum; eo iustius bellum gesturos."

The Samnites, now stripped of every advantage which gave

them the victory at Caudium, pathetically call for the

restoration of their former advantages and condemn the

Romans' trick to regain the gods' favor (11.1-13). They per-

ceive too late that they have squandered their opportunity

(12.1-2); the very ability to renew the war guarantees

victory for Roman arms (12.3-4):

> Adeoque nullodum certamine inclinatis uiri-
> bus post Caudinam pacem animi mutauerant, ut
> clariorem inter Romanos deditio Postumium
> quam Pontium incruenta uictoria inter Samnites
> faceret, et geri posse bellum Romani pro
> uictoria certa haberent, Samnites simul
> rebellasse et uicisse crederent Romanum.

When once the Romans have regained their traditional

character and the gods' favor, Caudium--the result exclu-

sively of special favors--can have no lingering effects upon

the war. The battle emerges from Livy's narrative not so

much as a Samnite victory as a prolegomenon to massive

Samnite defeats: so thoroughly does Livy emphasize the trans-

ience of the causes of the defeat, and so greatly does he

foreshadow the ultimate reversal of fortunes.

Several Samnite defeats ensue immediately, bearing out
the truth of their forebodings: in Samnium their Caudine
legions are defeated by Publilius (12.9-13.5); they are
slaughtered in battle near Luceria (14.6-16); they lose
Luceria itself, along with the hostages taken at Caudium,
to a Roman siege (15.3-8); finally, their garrison at Satricum is massacred (16.2-10). The theme of vengeance for
Caudium dominates these events. So eager are the Romans to
engage at 13.1-5 that they cast away their _pila_ and rush the
foe; their _ira_, not the general's skill, wins the day.[1] As
they storm the Samnite camp near Luceria they cry that the
Samnites will find no Caudine Forks or difficult passes to
aid them against Roman courage (14.10).[2] After the fall of
Luceria the garrison is sent under the yoke to avenge the
Roman humiliation (15.4-6).[3] Finally, after recovering the
Caudine hostages at Luceria (15.7), the Romans are even able--
according to some of Livy's sources--to complete their
"sudden reversal of fortune" (_mutatione subita rerum_) by
sending Pontius himself under the yoke (15.8). These victories expunge the humiliation of Caudium and are celebrated

---

[1] See especially 13.2-3.

[2] "...pro se quisque non haec Furculas nec Caudium nec
saltus inuios esse, ubi errorem fraus superbe uicisset, sed
Romanam uirtutem, quam nec uallum nec fossae arcerent,
memorantes caedunt pariter resistentes fususque...".

[3] "Iis Papirius ita respondit debuisse eos Pontium
Herenni filium, quo auctore Romanos sub iugum misissent,
consulere quid uictis patiendum censeret...militem se cum
singulis uestimentis sub iugum missurum, ulciscentem inlatam,
non nouam inferentem ignominiam."

with "the best-deserved triumph, save for Furius Camillus',
down to that day."[1]

The famous and lengthy digression on Alexander the
Great yet further expunges the shame of Caudium (IX.17-19).
It lauds the martial excellence of Roman commanders[2] and men
alike, finally judging that Alexander would have been defeated had he attacked westward against the Romans. This
digression, as Burck points out, diminishes the humiliation
of Caudium; more importantly, it serves as a "divider" which
isolates the disgrace from the rest of the book.[3] Directly
after the digression the Samnites, having implored the
Romans for peace, are permitted a two-year truce (20.1-3).

The war is quickly renewed (21.2), but Rome's conquests
proceed uninterrupted through the middle chapters of the
book.[4] At 21.2-22.11 Livy treats at length Rome's victories
outside Saticula, culminating finally in the surrender of the
town; the loss of Plistica to a Samnite assault is barely

---

[1]15.10: "...iustissimo triumpho ad eam aetatem secundum
Furium Camillum triumphauerit...".

[2]Note also the praise given Papirius Cursor's character
at 16.11-19.

[3]See Burck in Vom Menschenbild in der römischen Literatur,
ed. E. Lefèvre (Heidelberg 1966) 325: "Dann folgt eine Pause
und ein fast zeitloses Zwischenstück (17-19): der Vergleich
der Macht Alexanders des Grossen und Roms...--ein Nachweis,
der gerade an dieser Stelle sicherlich auch dem Zwecke
dient, die Schmach von Caudium zu isolieren und in ihrer
Auswirkung zu mindern."

[4]See Burck in Vom Menschenbild in der römischen Literatur,
ed. E. Lefèvre (Heidelberg 1966) 325: "In der Buchmitte
(20-28; Jh. 318-313)...der Eindruck von Roms wachsender
Überlegenheit immer beherrschender wird."

noted (22.11). More striking is Livy's gloss of the Romans'
defeat at Lautulae. He deals with the battle briefly and
chooses to regard it as a draw (23.4), relegating to a variant the tradition which recorded a Roman defeat (23.5).[1] Yet
he does not hesitate to chronicle at length a great Roman
victory (23.6-17) after the battle, even though the circumstances of the victory--the dictator is besieged in camp
(23.7), and the surrounding area is in revolt (23.10)--seem
predicated upon the versions which record a defeat at
Lautulae. Sora is betrayed to the Romans (24.1-15), as are
the Auruncan towns of Ausona, Minturnae, and Vescia (25.1-9).
Rebellious Luceria, having admitted a Samnite garrison, is
likewise reduced to obedience (26.1-2). Finally, the
Romans rout a Samnite army in the vicinity of Caudium itself
(27.1-14); after an action at Fregellae, they defeat the
Samnites again at Nola (28.3-6). The Romans thus establish
so clear a superiority over the Samnites that Livy says the
war's end seems to be at hand.[2]

Just at this moment, however, the report of war with
the Etruscans revives the dread of a terrible enemy (29.1-5).[3]
Through much of the rest of Book IX Livy emphasizes the

---

[1]Diodorus XIX.72.6-8 follows the variant tradition.

[2]29.1: "Profligato fere Samnitium bello..."; 29.3:
"...altero consule in Samnio reliquias belli persequente...".

[3]See 29.2: "...nec erat ea tempestate gens alia, cuius
secundum Gallicos tumultus arma terribiliora essent cum
propinquitate agri tum multitudine hominum."

gravity of Rome's peril against her two formidable enemies.[1]
This heightened danger, however, only magnifies the Romans'
achievement as Livy records their many victories over both
Etruscans and Samnites.

At 31.1-5 the Romans, incensed at the Samnites' cruelty
towards the garrison of Cluviae, easily recapture the town
and then proceed to take Bovianum. Unable to withstand the
Romans on a fair field (31.6), the Samnites attempt to lure
them into a trap. The ensuing battle, though somewhat difficult, is a decisive Roman victory, told in terms which again
expunge the shame of Caudium and emphasize the superiority of
the Roman soldier over the Samnite (31.6-16).[2] Rome then
wins another major victory by defeating the formidable[3]
Etruscan coalition at Sutrium, despite suffering heavy
casualties in the process (32.1-12). In the following year

---

[1]See, for example, 30.10: "Haec inter duorum ingentium
bellorum curam gerebantur."

[2]The preliminaries to the battle recall Caudium. At
31.6 the Samnites seek to lay an ambush; at 31.8 they
attack in a _saltus_. Even the planting of information at
31.7 parallels 2.2-4. Far different, however, is the Roman
reaction here (31.9) than at Caudium (2.10-3.4). The theme
of Livy's account is that the Romans are able to overcome
any disadvantage of terrain (31.13): "sed quem esse iam
uirtuti Romanae inexpugnabilem locum?" The consul cites, as
proof that terrain cannot resist their might, the recent
conquests of Sora and Fregellae, though we might note that
in fact the former was captured by a deserter's ploy
(24.3-10) and the latter was taken without a struggle (28.3).
Most importantly, the battle is decided as soon as the
Romans, fighting uphill, reach level ground; the Samnites
immediately turn and run (31.14-15). In avenging Caudium,
the Romans thus demonstrate convincingly their superiority
over the Samnite soldiers.

[3]32.1: "...iam omnes Etruriae populi praeter Arretinos
ad arma ierant...ingens orsi bellum."

the Romans engage another massive Etruscan army (35.2:
ingentem multitudinem) at Sutrium, and win an even greater
victory (35.1-8).[1] They then overcome another geographical
obstacle in crossing the Ciminian Forest[2] and devastating
the lands on the other side (36.1-14). Finally the Etruscans,
returning to Sutrium, mount their most serious threat so
far (37.1-2). This greater threat, however, is merely resolved into a greater Roman victory; legations from three
Etruscan cities accordingly seek peace (37.3-12).

As at 29.1-3, Livy again at 38.2-8 renews the sense of
tension in the account just when Rome's position seems
secure. Here he records a minor setback to a naval raid,
the Samnites' confident plans to combine forces with the
Etruscans, and even a marginal Samnite victory over the
Romans. The Samnites then face Rome as if anew; both sides
"feel confidence in their own strength, but without disdain
for the enemy."[3] Again, however, Roman victories follow the
build-up of tension; this time their magnitude is even
greater than before. The Etruscans,[4] fielding an army of

---

[1]In both battles, Roman uirtus overcomes the Etruscans'
numerical superiority (32.7, 35.3).

[2]The forest is described in fearful terms (36.1, 36.6).
The old dread of Caudium makes it even more terrible (36.1;
cf. 36.14).

[3]39.3: "...nec suis diffidentes uiribus nec hostem
spernentes...".

[4]We would expect, in the light of 39.1-3, to see battle
joined with the Samnites rather than the Etruscans. On the
vexed textual question of 39.4 see Walters and Conway ad loc.
A substantial lacuna in this place would, if accepted, render
problematic any judgment of the tempo of the whole passage.

picked men, fight so bitterly that the Romans seem to be facing a different foe. In a protracted and difficult struggle,
however, the outcome decisively favors the Romans: the
Etruscans' ancient power is broken on that day (39.5-11).[1]
The Samnites likewise exert themselves to the fullest, and
are similarly crushed. Livy describes their elaborate preparation of golden and silver armies for battle. Yet in an
ingens certamen the main struggle is among Romans, to see who
shall crush the enemy first and most decisively; victory is
won on a magnificent scale (40.1-17). After these victories
Rome easily dominates her enemies through the rest of the
book. Aside from several minor victories, she forces the
Etruscans to seek amicitia (40.20) and a foedus (41.6) and
defeats the Umbri (41.8-20), Hernici (43.2-7) and Aequi
(45.5-18). Most importantly, Rome inflicts several further
defeats upon the Samnites (42.6-8, 43.7-21, 44.5-15, 44.16);[2]
they ultimately sue for and receive peace (45.1-4). Rome's
military supremacy is thus unchallenged at the end of Book
IX.[3]

BOOK X

   Book X carries the tempo of Rome's expansion to a
suitable climax. Various unimportant battles near the start

---

[1]39.11: "Ille primum dies fortuna uetere abundantes
Etruscorum fregit opes...".

[2]The victory at 42.6-8 once more avenges the Caudine
defeat: the captured Samnites are sent under the yoke.

[3]Even here, certain discordant notes maintain the
reader's interest in events; see 41.11, 43.4-5.

of the book receive little emphasis. When hostilities are
resumed with the Samnites, however, the dramatic tempo picks
up. Tension builds to a climax at the decisive battle of
Sentinum; following her triumph there Rome "mops up" against
her weakened foes. As the pentad ends the Romans appear
invincibly established as the destined masters of Italy.

Sporadic operations at the beginning of Book X are of
little consequence. We may note that the Etruscans, taking
up arms, gain some initial successes against the Romans, but
are soon beaten decisively (3.6-5.12);[1] all of Rome's
enemies are then quiescent (6.1-2). We may likewise note
that the Etruscans later endeavor, without success, to bring
the Gauls into an attack upon the Romans (10.6-12); declaring
war anyway, they suffer badly from the depredations of the
consul Marcus Valerius (11.1-6).

With the beginning of the Third Samnite War, events
begin to be told with more dramatic emphasis. By contrast
with the previous two conflicts, however, there is little
stress here upon the opening of hostilities. The war is
foreshadowed only once (11.7-8) and then only virtually at
the start. More importantly, the circumstances surrounding
the declaration of war itself are told much more briefly than
on the previous two occasions (11.11-12.3). Within the
brief introductory section, however, Livy portrays this war

---

[1]In this battle Etruscan might is said to be broken for
the second time (5.12): "Hoc proelio fractae iterum
Etruscorum uires...". Their strength was first broken at
IX.39.11; above, 154-155.

as the result of Samnite provocation and guilt: they attack
the Lucani, persisting even after the latter's alliance with
Rome; further, they threaten violence against the Roman
fetiales. Two reasons explain the brevity of Livy's introduction to this war. First, the guilt of the Samnites was
so strongly established previously that there is now no need
to develop the issue at length. Beyond this, however, Livy's
purpose in this new war is essentially different than it
was at the start of the Second Samnite War. There, he
dramatically emphasized the Samnites' challenge for the rule
of Italy. Throughout Book X, Livy's coverage of the Third
Samnite War will stress that the challenge has been success-
fully met; his emphasis accordingly is not on the outbreak,
but rather the decisive victories of the war: the Battle
of Sentinum, followed by the rout of the Linen Legion and
finally, the easy conquest of enemy territories.

Immediately after the declaration of war, Livy begins
building up to the Battle of Sentinum. This decisive engagement is, along with the beginning of the Second Samnite War,
more extensively foreshadowed than any other event in the
entire pentad: an indication of its exceptional importance.
The foreshadowings, which occur at 13.2-4, 16.3-8, 18.1-2,
21.1-4, and 21.11-15, consistently emphasize the formation
of a grand international alliance against Rome, and the coming
of a great and difficult war. This emphasis is particularly
evident at 13.2-4 and 16.3-8, where Rome's increasing peril
is stressed in spite of some evidence to the contrary. In
the former case he stresses the great dangers of an Etruscan

and Samnite combination even though the next mention of the
Etruscans shows them seeking peace (14.3). In the latter
case the movement of a Samnite army into Etruria causes Livy
to emphasize Rome's dire peril once more, even though the
next chapter records Rome's easy conquest of three Samnite
towns (17.1-12). We may regard 16.3-8 as essentially a
duplicate of the notice of Rome's jeopardy at 18.1-2, and
superfluous for all purposes save one: it dramatizes the
general military crisis.

The account of the war's early events is only loosely
structured. Certain incidents, however, are linked to the
unifying topic of a great external military threat. These
help to foreshadow the Battle at Sentinum; becoming more
frequent as the battle draws closer, they cause the sense of
terror to increase as the dread showdown approaches. The
elections for 297 and 295, for example, both look forward to
the impending crisis (13.5, 21.13-15). Likewise, the notice
of Rome's peril at 18.1-2 lends urgency to her difficulties
at 18.5-6. It is the threat to Rome which also causes the
army to appeal for Volumnius' assistance in Etruria at
19.1-4 and 19.10-12.[1]

By virtue of its extensive foreshadowing and the strong
tempo of danger which grows as the battle approaches, the
Battle of Sentinum appears as the decisive struggle between
Rome and her host of enemies. Livy's treatment of the battle

---

[1]The dramatic tension increases in spite of two Roman
victories: over a combined army of Samnites and Etruscans
(19.14-22), and over a Samnite force (20.3-16).

itself also indicates its supreme importance. Four factors mark the battle as a decisive moment in the war: the great length of Livy's account,[1] the description of both sides' massive efforts to indicate that Sentinum is the "all-out" showdown, the extremity of danger, and of course the decisive victory achieved by Rome in the battle.[2]

That the battle represents Rome's greatest effort is implicit in the debate on the forces required for such a war (25.11-18) and in the decision to send Decius to Etruria (26.1-4). Livy gives details about the great force of Romans, Latins, and allies at 26.14-15.[3] The massive foreshadowing of the engagement has already indicated that Sentinum represents the greatest effort of the enemy host. Livy further refers to a "great multitude" (26.7: multitudine ingenti) of Senonian Gauls who overwhelm Scipio's force at Clusium; so large is the enemy coalition that the Gauls and Samnites camp separately from the Etruscans and Umbrians (27.2-3). Thus Sentinum appears as the maximum effort of each side.

Certain scattered references to Rome's peril also underline the gravity of the situation. Admittedly, Fabius

---

[1] Events surrounding the battle, plus the battle itself, require ten pages in the Teubner text.

[2] The battle's importance is also demonstrated by the appearance of an omen just before the armies clash; it indicates that the Gauls will be slaughtered and put to flight (27.8-9).

[3] At 27.10-11 we learn that the first, third, fifth, and sixth legions are at Sentinum; the second and fourth are campaigning in Samnium.

seems confident when he joins his army at 25.1-4, and accepts
rather than requires the aid of Decius at 26.1-4. The Roman
people also feel greatly confident after Decius' appointment
to Etruria (26.4).[1] The danger of Rome's position, however,
remains manifest. Decius refers to the war as "harsh and
difficult" (24.12: asperum ac difficile) and as a "danger"
(24.14: periculum). Appius Claudius sends an alarming report
of the situation in Etruria (24.18); his own terror, and
that of his soldiers, is vividly portrayed (25.5-9). Rome's
peril is clearly developed in the debate on the forces
needed for the war (25.13-14).[2] The defeat of Scipio by the
Senonian Gauls (26.7-13) emphasizes further the crisis;
Livy speaks of the year's "especial terror" (26.13: praecipuus
terror) of Gallic unrest.[3] Fortunately for the Romans, they
are able by a bold foray to divert the Etruscans, and apparently the Umbrians, to the defense of the area around Clusium
(27.5-6).[4] It is Livy's opinion that only their success in

---

[1]Surely dramatic necessity accounts at least in part for
Fabius' confidence. Livy, having described Fabius' quarrel
for sole command in Etruria, can hardly portray him as feel-
ing inadequate to the situation there. Likewise, the popular
confidence at the appointment of Decius may be explained on
thematic grounds; it underlines the value of harmony.

[2]"...[Ap. Claudius] terrorem belli Etrusci augeret:
non suffecturum ducem unum nec exercitum unum aduersus
quattuor populos; periculum esse, siue iuncti unum premant
siue diuersi gerant bellum, ne ad omnia simul obire unus
non possit."

[3]Livy could have adopted a source which recounted a more
favorable outcome (26.12). Yet a Roman defeat here builds
tension for the Battle of Sentinum; most importantly, Livy
considered the account of the defeat to be more likely (26.13).

[4]Livy does not say that the Umbrians withdrew from
Sentinum with the Etruscans, but they are not listed in the

dividing the enemy's force saves the Romans from disaster at
Sentinum (27.11): "Primo concursu adeo aequis uiribus gesta
res est ut, si adfuissent Etrusci et Vmbri aut in acie aut in
castris, quocumque se inclinassent, accipienda clades fuerit."

Livy continues to stress Rome's dire peril during the
actual engagement. This he does by portraying events on
Decius' wing as decisive. After Decius expends his energies
in an initial assault, his cavalry are thrown back in terror.
Their panic spreads to the infantry; the whole wing is hard
pressed by the enemy (28.6-11). In this crisis Decius, by
devoting himself (28.12-18), causes an almost miraculous
turn in Rome's fortunes. Suddenly the Gauls, having lost
their faculties, fight only ineffectively; the Romans restore
the situation and begin to slaughter the foe (29.1-7). The
less exciting events on Fabius' wing are clearly secondary:
his plan to delay a decision (28.2-5) is told as a prelude to
Decius' attack, while his successful attack against the
Samnite contingent has only a minor peripeteia (29.9-10).
His success merely continues the success achieved on Decius'
wing. By organizing the narrative in this fashion Livy emphasizes not only Decius' devotio but the extreme danger
incurred by Rome in the battle.

At Sentinum, as frequently in Livy,[1] the decisiveness
of the battle is proportionate to the danger incurred. He

---

order of battle at 27.10, and at 27.11 are specifically said
to have been absent.

[1]See above, 135.

describes a vast slaughter of the enemy on both wings, including the capture of the Samnite camp and the death of
their general, Gellius Egnatius (29.1-16); at 29.17-18
he lists 25,000 enemies killed with 8000 captured against
8700 Romans slain. The decisiveness of the victory is
further marked by the honors given Decius (29.18-20), by
Fabius' magnificent triumph in Rome (30.8-10), and by Livy's
comment that any unexaggerated account of the battle is
glorious enough (30.4-5).

Rome's victory over the enemy coalition at Sentinum
breaks the back of Italian resistance. Livy notes the
Samnites' desperation at 31.6, and at 31.10´-15 details, with
great admiration for their steadfast courage, their impossible
plight (31.12-14):[1]

> ...proximo anno Samnites in Sentinati agro, in
> Paelignis, ad Tifernum, Stellatibus campis, suis
> ipsi legionibus, mixti alienis, ab quattuor
> exercitibus, quattuor ducibus Romanis caesi
> fuerant; imperatorem clarissimum gentis suae
> amiserant; socios belli, Etruscos, Vmbros,
> Gallos, in eadem fortuna uidebant qua ipsi
> erant; nec suis nec externis uiribus iam stare
> poterant, tamen bello non abstinebant. Adeo
> ne infeliciter quidem defensae libertatis
> taedebat et uinci quam non temptare uictoriam
> malebant.

Livy's tribute is, in effect, the epitaph for serious
Italian resistance in the pentad. Thereafter, in spite of
certain minor threats[2] by Rome's enemies, the overwhelming

---

[1]Not even the historian's free admission that the war
will continue to drag on (31.10) diminishes the impact of
Rome's supremacy over the Samnites.

[2]For example, 31.2, 32.2, 33.7, 35.1-3, 45.4-5, and 45.12.
All of these threats are quickly countered by the Romans.

emphasis is on the ease with which Rome conquers and the desperation of her foes. At 32.2 Livy never raises the specter of the formidable enemy coalition, even though the Samnites reportedly intend to send an army to Etruria. At 32.5-33.6 the Samnites boldly attack the Roman camp and inflict several hundred casualties; yet Livy sees the incident not as a threat to the Roman cause[1] but as a proof of the Samnites' desperation (32.5): "...ausi Samnites sunt--tantum desperatio ultima temeritatis facit--castra Romana oppugnare...".

After recounting various Roman successes at 33.7-34.14, Livy recounts another major action at length at 35.1-36.15. After an initial encounter in which the Samnites defeat the Romans (35.1-3) the two sides fight a more important battle on the following day (35.4-36.15). In this highly stylized engagement, organized around the theme of faintheartedness,[2] the decisive moment comes when the Romans, faced with defeat, cast off their faintness (36.6-12). They then easily reverse the fortunes of the battle (36.12) and surround and destroy the foe (36.13-14). Livy recounts heavy casualties on both

---

[1] Livy grants the audacity of the attack, but never concedes more than a limited victory to the attacker (32.5): "...quamquam non uenit ad finem tam audax inceptum, tamen haud omnino uanum fuit." At 33.7 he terms it "non infelix audacia."

[2] See, for example, 36.3: "Neutris animus est ad pugnandum, diuersique integri atque intacti abissent, ni cedenti instaturum alterum timuissent. Sua sponte inter inuitos tergiuersantesque segnis pugna clamore incerto atque impari coepit; nec uestigio quisquam mouebatur."

sides (36.14-15).[1] More victories follow: over the Samnites
(36.16-17), who are clearly on the verge of defeat;[2] and in
Etruria, where three very powerful cities seek peace (37.1-5).

Finally, the series of victories climaxes in the rout of
the Linen Legion (38.1-42.7). While this battle lacks the
foreshadowing or dramatic tension which marked Sentinum as a
turning point, the massive effort to raise the Linen Legion
indicates that this engagement represents the full extent of
the Samnites' power. Livy shows that their best men,
elaborately accoutered, have been prepared for the struggle
(38.1-13). He impressively describes the horrible ceremony
and dire oath which bind them to fight to the death rather
than flee (38.5-12).[3] It is clear, however, that the
Samnites are no match for the Romans. Papirius' address to
his troops (39.11-17) cleverly reverses the reader's earlier
impressions of both the Samnites' weapons and dire oaths.
Their armament, earlier a token of their massive effort, now

---

[1]The battle's dominant theme of faintheartedness perhaps
ill suits the general trend of Roman might and supremacy.
Livy of course must often record facts which do not fit in
with overall historical trends. Yet it is most unusual for
him, when describing an episode in his own literary terms,
to describe it in a way so much at variance with the larger
historical trend.

[2]37.1: "...in Samnitibus materia belli deerat...".

[3]Livy further indicates the battle's importance in his
general treatment of the narrative. He foregoes his usual
practice of naming both consuls at the beginning of their
consular year in order to focus on Papirius and his coming
great victory. Papirius is introduced at 38.1; his colleague
Carvilius, not until 39.1. Furthermore even Carvilius, who
is besieging Cominium, is more intent upon Papirius' battle
than upon his own (39.7).

seems but a weak and idle display (39.11-14). And their
unholy oaths, undertaken in violation of treaty, now seem only
to inflict them with fear alike of their gods, fellow-citizens,
and enemies (39.15-17). In contrast to this picture of weakness and demoralization, the Romans clamor eagerly for
battle (40.1-4). Livy then describes the Romans' receipt of
favorable auspices in spite of the sin of a pullarius
(40.4-14), as well as a stratagem for the battle: Spurius
Nautius will take mules to all nearby hills in simulation of
cavalry (40.8). Thus on the verge of battle the Romans are
portrayed as powerful, confident, and divinely favored. The
Samnites, in spite of all their efforts, seem weak,[1]
terror-stricken, and baneful to the gods. Indeed, the
numbing fear which grips the Samnites is everywhere apparent
at 41.1-4, where the battle is joined. The result of their
fear is an instant massacre; they fight only sluggishly and
are cut down, though they refuse at first to flee (41.4):
"Instare Romanus a cornu utroque, a media acie et caedere
deorum hominumque attonitos metu; repugnatur segniter, ut ab
iis quos timor moraretur a fuga." The peripeteia of the battle therefore does not consist in a reversal of fortune.
Rather, this initial massacre is turned into a rout by the
use of Nautius' stratagem (41.5-9). The vigorous follow-up
to the battle, wherein the Romans capture the enemy camp and
the town of Aquilonia, again emphasizes the Samnites' weakness

---

[1]At 41.2 Livy describes them as per aliquot iam annos
uinci adsueti. By contrast, at 35.2 he says of the Romans:
insueti erant uinci.

(41.10-42.4). A motif of the narrative has been their various fears which restrain them from flight. Hence now, in flight, they fear none but the Romans (41.10): "...nec quemquam praeter hostes metuunt." Likewise their brief success in defending Aquilonia is specifically attributed to the walls of the town, not the defenders' courage (41.12). By contrast, the Romans are still avid for combat (41.13-14). Finally, Livy ends the account by citing the Samnites' disastrous losses (42.5)[1] and briefly sketching the character of Papirius, whose eagerness and confidence in battle (42.6-7) are emblematic of the entire Roman army.

Livy has thus made the battle with the Linen Legion a major episode. The massiveness of the Samnites' effort, combined with their utter defeat in battle,[2] indicates how completely Samnium has been overmatched by Rome. And Livy has reinforced this effect by contrasting their fear with the confidence of the Romans.[3]

Roman forces continue to display absolute supremacy over the foe through the rest of the book. At 43.1-8 they capture Cominium, where the Samnites are said to be no match for the Romans in close combat or on equal terrain (43.5-6). At

---

[1]They lose 20,340 killed, and suffer the capture of 3870 men and ninety-seven military standards.

[2]See 38.1: "Sequitur hunc annum...et bellum ingens uictoriaque quantam de Samnitibus nemo ad eam diem praeter L. Papirium patrem consulis pepererat."

[3]Stadter, Historia 21 (1972) 294 has noted the importance of this battle as an assertion of Roman supremacy.

43.9-15 some twenty intact Samnite cohorts,[1] in great trep-
idation, flee under harassment to Bovianum. At 44.6-8 the
Samnites are clearly at Rome's mercy. They seem to have
abandoned regular field operations; only the storming of
cities remains.[2] After some trouble with the Etruscans
(45.2-8) Livy cites various Roman successes in Samnium
(45.9-14) and Etruria (46.10-12). Already, the lavish award
of military decorations (44.3-5) and the holding of a four
days' supplicatio (45.1) would seem to indicate that the war
is nearly won.[3] Now the grand triumphs of Papirius (46.1-9)
and Carvilius (46.13-15) end the account of military affairs
on an unmistakable note: Rome is completely and everywhere
triumphant over her enemies.

CONCLUSIONS

Livy's treatment of the military narrative demonstrates
the same dramatic "pace" which marked his handling of the
struggle of the orders. Again, major scenes are largely

---

[1]The number of cohorts is given in earlier references to
these troops at 40.6 and 43.2.

[2]"Consilium inde habitum [cum] iamne tempus esset
deducendi ab Samnio exercitus aut utriusque aut certe
alterius; optimum uisum, quo magis fractae res Samnitium
essent, eo pertinacius et infestius agere cetera et persequi
ut perdomitum Samnium insequentibus consulibus tradi posset:
quando iam nullus esset hostium exercitus qui signis conlatis
dimicaturus uideretur, unum superesse belli genus, urbium
oppugnationes, quarum per excidia militem locupletare praeda
et hostem pro aris ac focis dimicantem conficere possent."

[3]At 45.5, where the Romans warn that the Etruscans will
soon meet the same fate as the Samnites, the clear implication
is that the Samnites have been beaten.

responsible for indicating the direction of events. In
Books VI and VII, however, domestic affairs dominate; Rome's
minor wars are treated with little elaboration. Even the
account of the First Samnite War creates little impression
of Roman expansion; instead, it draws the character of the
opponents and seeks to justify Rome's intervention in
Campania. Nor does the tempo pick up early in Book VIII.
After the defeat of the Latin Rebellion, however, two speeches
indicate that Rome, by treating her defeated neighbors
generously, will secure an enduring empire for herself. These
speeches, which conclude the pentad's first half, show that
Rome has consolidated her local conquests. Immediately, the
outbreak of the Second Samnite War sets a strong interpretive
framework for succeeding events: the issue at stake in Rome's
wars will be the mastery of all Italy. This issue dominates
the pentad's second half. By the end of Book VIII Rome has
made visible progress towards her goal of peninsular hegemony.
First, the people of Tarentum fear that her success against
the Samnites will extend her power over all Italy. Further,
the book ends on a strong dramatic note as Cornelius inflicts
a severe defeat upon the Samnites. Books IX and X continue
the strong dramatic movement towards growing domination over
the Samnites and Italy. This overall intention is strikingly
evident in the treatment of the Caudine disaster. Livy
constantly emphasizes that this defeat was incurred only
because of special factors: terrain, the gods' anger, poor
generalship, and even the Romans' loss of character. Further,

he constantly stresses that Rome will avenge herself of a
fair field. In his hands, therefore, Caudium appears not so
much as a defeat as a prelude to great Roman victories.
Thereafter, Book IX amply records Rome's vengeance for Caudium.
A series of great victories, culminating in the rout of the
Samnites' gold and silver armies, forces the Samnites to beg
for peace as the book ends. Book X carries this dramatic
movement to a suitable climax. After the resumption of
hostilities, Rome decisively defeats the Samnites and their
allies in the middle of the book at Sentinum. Livy even comments, in the aftermath of this defeat, that their continued
resistance is useless. Still more defeats ensue, culminating
in the destruction of the Linen Legion. As the pentad ends
the Romans, absolutely supreme in the field, appear destined
to be the masters of Italy.

We should note one further technique of presentation by
which Livy secures the proper dramatic impact for Rome's
growing power. Book XI will begin with a reversal: the
Samnites' victory over Fabius Gurges.[1] Such a defeat could
easily spoil the impression, so assiduously cultivated in
Books VI-X, of Rome's power. Livy faced the same problem in
Book VIII, where his portrayal of Rome's military strength
would be ill served by the fact that Book IX began with the
Caudine Forks.[2] There his solution was not to foreshadow the
defeat. Here, he adopts the same solution; he gives no hint

---

[1]See above, 20.

[2]See above, 138-139.

in Book X whatsoever that Rome is about to suffer a defeat in
Book XI.

We have also seen that Livy creates, at the center of
the pentad, a strong moral statement of the reasons for Rome's
growing strength: fair treatment of allies and military discipline. Furthermore, the treatment of Papirius Cursor and
Fabius Rullianus demonstrates that Livy is concerned in their
quarrel to explore proper military discipline, not the
characters of the men.

CHAPTER THREE

THE LITERARY HISTORIAN

Livy has come under attack at times for attempting to
deceive and mislead his readers with flagrant misrepresenta-
tions of fact. His account of the Caudine Forks, for example,
is said to be "fictitiously reconstructed with a face-saving
theological framework and a structure more appropriate to
drama than to historical narrative."[1] We have indeed seen
many cases where Livy casts verisimilitude to the wind; often
his purpose is to make a larger point by sacrificing
verisimilitude in matters of detail. At Caudium, for example,
the Romans cannot even come to grips with the Samnites;
equally incredible is the loss and recovery of their proper
character. Through this method Livy stresses that Caudium is
merely an aberration from the dominant trend of Roman
conquest. The treatment of individual characters is similar.
Quinctius has no share in his own conspiracy so that he may
be a symbol of modestia. Decius and Fabius are divorced from
their own quarrel over provincial assignments so that their
conflict may be seen as one between the orders. Most
incredible of all are Papirius and Fabius, whose characters
bear artificiality on their very face. And yet the highly
stylized account of their dispute brings out an important

---

[1]Walsh, Livy 281.

lesson about military discipline.

It is important to note that Livy does not in these
cases attempt to conceal the artificiality of his account.
Indeed, he often emphasizes it. His narratives of Caudium
and the quarrel of Papirius and Fabius both pivot structurally around the most unbelievable aspects of the stories. So
does the battle fought under the joint command of Camillus
and L. Furius Medullinus. The battle at X.35.4-36.15, in
which both sides are faint of heart, is patently unreal.
This is hardly the work of a man attempting to deceive his
readers.

Livy's attitude towards the historical tradition of
these early times has been perceptively assessed by Luce.[1]
Livy was fully aware that the details of Rome's early history
lay beyond his ability to discern--as they lie beyond ours.
The problem was worst before the Gallic sack (VI.1.1-3), but
even the period thereafter posed many problems which could
never be solved (VII.6.6): "Cura non deesset, si qua ad uerum
uia inquirentem ferret: nunc fama rerum standum est, ubi cer-
tam derogat uetustas fidem...". In this situation there was
no fault in the historian who confessed his ignorance of the
truth. The fault lay in the all too easy pretense of knowledge where no sure knowledge existed. Certainly it was for
this reason that he reserved particular scorn for Valerius
Antias, whose daring went so far as to record the precise
casualties of an early battle (III.5.12-13). Livy put no

---

[1]TAPhA 102 (1971) 297-302.

such false front on events. The patent incredibility of
Livy's narrative at many points is designed in the first instance as an admission that factual details often are not to
be considered reliable. But it achieves more than that. By
molding the narrative as he does he is able to bring out the
larger trends which he did discern: the growth of Rome, the
acceptance of plebeian magistrates, the growing harmony of
the orders.[1] And various characters and episodes provide, as
Livian scholarship has often pointed out, useful illustrations
of the spirit of early Rome.

The liberties which he felt justified in taking with the
history of this period would seem to extend also to his use
of the sources. While any assessment of the way Livy handled
his sources in Books VI-X must be speculative, it seems very
possible that he sometimes chose one source over another because it fit in with the overall development which he sought
to emphasize. We have noted several cases where Livy follows
one source over a variant which, while he advances no specific
objections to it, would seemingly have been less suitable to
his purpose. For example, he rejected one source which removed Valerius, the great symbol of moderation, from any role
in ending the military conspiracy of 342 (VII.42.3-6). Again
it may well have been his desire to focus on domestic strife
in the quarrel of Decius and Fabius that guided his choice of

---

[1]The bold devices--unbelievable events and characters--
are hardly to be found in the later books: a significant indication that he did in fact strive to write a history reliable even in detail.

which version to follow. He rejected both those sources
which mentioned no quarrels at all and those which recorded
so many quarrels that there would be no clear focus on the
important dispute (X.26.5-6). Finally Livy saw Rome as a
model of fair and mild treatment after the Latin Rebellion.
Accordingly he adopted a version which recorded kind treatment of Fundi in this period, rejecting Claudius who recorded
much harsher treatment (VIII.19.13-14).[1]

Livy apparently felt justified in choosing one source
over another because it suited his purposes--but only in
cases where there was no way of discerning which was more
likely to be true. Livy followed sources which reported un-
pleasant facts if there was reason to prefer them to pleas-
anter versions. He reports poisonings in Rome even though
at least one source disagreed with the report (VIII.18.2-3).
He reports a Roman defeat instead of a victory because he
considered the defeat to be more likely. His attitude of
course falls far short of modern standards. But it is doubtful whether his approach was disreputable by the standards of
his own day.[2]

Livy has cast both of the pentad's great historical
trends into a common dramatic form that emphasizes the forward
"movement" of events. In both domestic and military issues,
grave problems face Rome as Book VI begins. Both are

---

[1]See above, 65 n.1, 84 n.1, 107 n.1.

[2]See the discussion in Luce, *Livy* 139-184, especially
147-158.

progressively resolved during the pentad. Both enjoy a
full-scale dramatic climax in Book X where the major historical issues are brought to a grand resolution.[1]

We have already seen many of the devices by which Livy
shaped individual scenes to create his overall dramatic form.
It remains to discuss here a few general techniques which
will illustrate how thoroughly he commanded his historical
facts as he composed, and how greatly the historical trends
depend on literary technique.

The significant juxtaposition in Book VIII of Rome's
decision to grant citizenship with the beginning of the
"national" conquest is an example of Livy's overriding control of his material. To achieve this contrast Livy had to
treat several earlier events in particular ways. First, to
emphasize the importance of citizenship at this particular
point he deliberately offered little comment on the earlier
grants of citizenship to Tusculum (VI.26.8) and to certain
Veientes, Capenates, and Faliscans (VI.4.4). In so doing he
perhaps deviated from what he found in some of his sources;
Dionysius of Halicarnassus at any rate discusses the policy's

---

[1]The third decade, Livy's only other extant unit which
is strongly dramatic, shows a similar forward movement.
Rome's terrible defeats against Hannibal are dramatized in
Books XI-XXII. The war's middle phase, less intense dramatically, shows the gradual shift of momentum over the next
six books. Carthage seems ascendant through Book XXV;
thereafter, the dramatic and historical advantage swings
more and more to Rome in XXVI-XXVIII. Dramatic tempo picks
up for the grand climax in XXIX-XXX as Rome invades Africa
and brings the war to a successful conclusion. See Burck,
Einführung in die dritte Dekade des Livius (Heidelberg 1950)
7-56; idem in Livy, ed. T. A. Dorey (London and Toronto 1971)
21-26.

importance in the case of Tusculum (XIV.6). Likewise it would perhaps have seemed the obvious course to have taken the First, not the Second, Samnite War as the point of departure for Rome's ambitions to peninsular rule; certainly Livy is aware of the earlier war's importance (VII.29.1-2). By also deferring mention of peninsular conquest until the Second Samnite War Livy was able to show that the extension of citizenship directly enabled Rome to expand.[1]

The exposition of the plebeians' merit during Decius' speech for the Ogulnian Law also shows overall control and shaping on Livy's part. Their merit is demonstrated only when events build to a dramatic climax in X. This effect results particularly from the fact that Livy deliberately said very little about their proving their merit in earlier books--even in contexts where he might well have made such comments. Books VIII and IX especially had little to say on merit. And yet (as Decius points out: X.7.3-6, 8.1-4) plebeians in fact gave proof of their religious worth as long ago as 367 (VI.42.2) when they became decemviri sacris faciundis, and 340 (VIII.6.9-13, 9.1-12) when Decius' devotio pleased the gods. Indeed, the successful vota of many plebeian magistrates constantly demonstrated their worth throughout the period.

Livy's control over facts and large-scale issues can also be seen in his selection of some relatively minor

---

[1]The procedure is very similar to the "point-counterpoint" technique which Livy applied to the case of Popilius. See above, 54-56.

incidents as turning points for major themes or trends. We
have seen several cases where he reads enormous implications
into apparently insignificant episodes. The quarrel of
Decius and Fabius, to cite just one example, appears as the
pentad's final episode of domestic strife. The reconciliation
of the two men symbolizes the reconciliation of the two orders;
Decius' noble sacrifice at Sentinum proves the merits of
plebeian magistrates in general. The particular interpretation given to this incident in the middle of X is largely
responsible for creating the dramatic resolution of the issues
of harmony and merit in that book.

Any general assessment of Livy as historian must consider not only his perception of general trends but also his
identification of the turning points within the trends. How
valid are these turning points? Do they really correspond to
major shifts in the important historical trends? Do the
sudden turning points of the dramatic narrative show that
Livy saw changes in the direction of history as equally
sudden, abrupt, and easily identifiable? Or does his conception allow for slower, subtler developments over time
whose effects are cumulative and cannot be tied closely to
a single event? Finally, what causes underlay the great
historical developments?

Some of the turning-points--generally those which deal
with political decisions or military actions--do indeed mark
sudden and major shifts in the trends of Roman history. It
was precisely to mark such an important shift that Livy so

carefully emphasized the importance of citizenship in VIII.
Likewise, he realized clearly that no serious bid for peninsular hegemony could begin until the Latins had been brought
to Rome's side. It was the Second Samnite War therefore
which saw Rome strike out towards this goal. Nonetheless
the First Samnite War was important in its own right; it did
initiate, as Livy pointed out (VII.29.1-2), a long series of
wars against great foes. Livy stressed the decisive results
obtained by the victory at Sentinum (X.31.10-15). The resolution of the military conspiracy of 342 is unusual among the
decisive events, for it depends--more than any of the other
specific turning points--upon Livy's assigning a great moral
change to a fixed moment in history. Why did Livy assign
the learning of modestia and moderatio to a single event?
The answer, I believe, lies in what Livy found in his
historical sources. They clearly recorded that the
patricians occupied both consulships as late as 343--a thing
which to Livy represented usurpation of power, a grave
affront to the whole plebeian class. And yet his sources
attested few examples of class strife after the conspiracy
of 342 (IX.33.3). This was clear testimony that Romans
lacked these virtues earlier, and possessed them later.
Livy consequently found it most plausible to assign the
great moral development to the happy resolution of the military conspiracy in 342.

Livy believed, however, that many changes in Rome
occurred more slowly. Even though he links these changes to

particular episodes in the narrative, it seems best to consider those episodes simply as exemplars of an ongoing
historical process. They are not important turning points in
their own right. The demonstration of plebeian merit, for
example, took place not just at the Ogulnian Law but over
many years--as the account clearly indicated. The revelation
of their worth in one scene does not mean that Livy believed
the development to be a sudden one; it indicates only that he
regarded the development as important and wanted to develop
it dramatically.[1] Livy shows the patricians' acceptance of
plebeian worth after the quarrel of Decius and Fabius. Did
Livy believe the patricians' acceptance of plebeian merits
came at one fell stroke after the quarrel of Decius and
Fabius? Or did he think that acceptance developed more
gradually? Specific evidence is lacking, but the whole narrative has long shown the intensity of the patricians'
objections--and the intensity of the whole domestic struggle--
much reduced. The imperium Manlianum provides another
example of such a scene; it is considered just one example
of old-style severity in military discipline. Likewise the
quarrel of Papirius and Fabius, which shows that Roman commanders learn the need for moderation, is by no means the
first such case of moderation. The elder Fabius points to
Cincinnatus and Camillus as examples of the fine and moderate
exercise of command (VIII.33.13-16). Livy probably did

---

[1]He explicitly shows that the passage of time is important in establishing the plebeians' merits (X.8.11); see
above, 75.

believe that the case of Papirius represented an important
example of moral learning in Rome. He certainly entertained
no illusion, however, that the learning of moderation in
command sprang full-blown from this one incident. He simply
chose to emphasize the way Manlius and Papirius exercised
command, and to play the two cases off in counterpoint to
each other. He thereby gave pointed expression to a change
of disciplinary habits which had been in the making for many
years.

Livy has created, therefore, a narrative whose strong
dramatic pace points up several definite turning points and
climaxes. These show vividly not only the easily identifiable watersheds of history but the culmination of other
trends which Livy saw developing more slowly and less per-
ceptibly. It is particularly unsurprising that Livy should
see major historical changes developing almost imperceptibly
through time. He saw morals as critically important in
history, and knew that moral changes are accomplished only
over a long time. The passage of time, for example, was a
critical factor in the preparation of early Romans for the
responsibilities of freedom (II.1.2-6). Similarly the
dissolution of Rome's moral fabric, once it had been forged,
required a long time (Preface 9): "...labente deinde paulatim
disciplina uelut desidentes primo mores sequatur [quisque]
animo...".

The causes which Livy saw behind the great historical
developments of VI-X--domestic concord and Rome's military

supremacy--are overtly moralistic. A solution for the
domestic struggle particularly required moral learning. In
early Rome domestic tranquillity was enforced by the kings;[1]
foreign military threats also repressed the struggle from
time to time in the early republic. The domestic peace
which Rome now gains in VI-X--a peace which can hold firm
even without a king or foreign threats--is based exclusively
on the citizens' mastery of the social virtues of moderatio,
modestia, and mutual respect. The military expansion is of
course due largely to the skill of Rome's commanders and the
excellence of her fighting men, which is well epitomized by
Manlius at VII.9.6-10.14. In expansion too, however, moral
qualities play a basic and important role. The growth of
Roman power requires the largeness of mind to extend citizenship to her allies--an attitude that would have been unthinkable earlier.[2] Equally important is a new humane attitude
behind military discipline. Roman soldiers fight best under
a discipline which recognizes their dignity as men.

In his Preface Livy asks the reader to pay attention to
the critical role played by morals in his history (Preface
9): "...ad illa mihi pro se quisque acriter intendat animum,
quae uita, qui mores fuerint, per quos uiros quibusque artibus domi militiaeque et partum et auctum imperium sit...".
This exhortation has been almost universally understood to

---

[1]See above, 29-30.

[2]Spurius Cassius' overtures to the allies alienated
the citizens (II.41.8): "Cassius...in agraria largitione
ambitiosus in socios eoque ciuibus uilior erat...".

mean that he regards history as little more than a panorama
of men and their deeds, both good and bad.[1] While it is no
doubt true that he regarded individual exempla as important,
I believe he is referring at a deeper and more important
level to the whole Roman people, and to those acquired
qualities of toleration and respect which lay at the heart
of Rome's greatness. Indeed, Livy regards both the growing
harmony of Roman society and her increasing military success
as the natural fruits of these learned virtues.

Livy's view of history has been frequently condemned as
naive. Admittedly he never held public office; he did not
understand the decision-making process as well as many other
historians. It is characteristic that we do not find in him
mechanical explanations for events, such as Polybius' famous
analysis which attributes Rome's success to her excellent
constitutional system. Does Livy's moralistic view of
historical causation deserve to be condemned? I would
suggest that it does not. At one level, Livy inherited a
tradition which attested that for centuries the state had
been torn into rival camps by deeply felt enmity. If Romans
healed a division of this magnitude, surely the historian
did not err if he attributed the healing, in the end, to the
moral learning of men. At another level, Livy's moralistic

---

[1]See, for example, Walsh, Livy 82 who cites this passage
in connection with the statement that "Livy regards history as
pre-eminently concerned with individuals, especially with
leaders of communities; and in his analysis of their achievements and failures he draws attention to the moral attributes
or defects which he considers solely responsible for such
eventualities."

concerns address many general and specific policies of
statecraft.[1] Concerns very much like his are quite in
evidence today. We consider it an educational process if
blacks and whites learn to live together and accept each
other in racial harmony, or if Egypt and Israel try to
replace hatred with respect by exchanging trade, tourists,
and cultural groups. Those who promote these processes we
call statesmen. But the public learning process behind
racial and international peace represents a change within
the minds and hearts of men: a moral change. Livy, above
all ancient historians, understood that such changes greatly
overshadow the acts and decisions of political leaders. The
view that morals exercise a decisive effect on a people's
fortunes was therefore neither naive nor romantic,[2] and it is
unsurprising that it penetrated to the highest levels of
government. Indeed, Augustus' moral program was almost
certainly influenced to some degree by the moral outlook of

---

[1]Livy was surely aware that his history could provide
guidance for the statesman. He says that the study of the
past offers examples which an individual can choose to imitate
for himself (i.e., examples of personal conduct) and for the
republic (i.e., guidance for policies) (Preface 10): "Hoc
illud est praecipue in cognitione rerum salubre ac frugiferum,
omnis te exempli documenta in inlustri posita monumento
intueri; inde tibi tuaeque rei publicae quod imitere capias,
inde foedum inceptu foedum exitu quod uites." At XXV.33.6
he even advises future commanders not to let foreign auxili-
aries outnumber their Roman contingents. Such a statement,
however, is exceptional. And his general tendency to
simplify complex or specialized material, rightly noted by
Walsh, Livy 162, cautions us not to press this aspect of
his work too far.

[2]For this view see Syme, The Roman Revolution (Oxford
1939) 485-486.

writers like Livy. The first decade of Livy provided ready
models for Augustus' revival of archaic religious practices,
his laws to foster the values of marriage and to discourage
adultery, his official encouragement for bearing children,
and his policy of gaining wide Italian support for Rome.

It would lie beyond the scope of this study to examine
at length Livy's treatment of historical developments in
the later books.[1] We should note, however, that an examination of them reveals that Livy was not committed to a single
moralistic idea controlling all history; his explanation of
historical change is neither doctrinaire nor rigidly
schematic. In the third decade, for example, while the
excellence of the Roman people surely aids their cause
against Hannibal, it is the choice of strategies, not moral
learning, which lies at the dramatic heart of the narrative.
The appropriate strategy is, in Livy's view, itself dependent
primarily on such factors as manpower and supplies. The
defeat of Antiochus in the eighth pentad is attributable to
specific decisions like his failure to secure the support of
King Philip V, the inadequate size of his expedition to
Greece, his withdrawal from Lysimachia, and the defeat of
his navy at Myonnesus--all of which prepared the way for his
later defeat at Magnesia.

Examination of the later books also reveals little

---

[1]An examination of the historical changes, the causes
behind them, and literary techniques in the later books may
be found in my forthcoming essay, "Livy," in Ancient Writers:
Greece and Rome, ed. T. J. Luce (New York). On the moral
decline see Luce, Livy 250-275.

systematic concern with moral issues until Books XXXVII-XLV.[1]
The later books recount the opening stages of Rome's moral
decline: the shocking effects of Asian wealth and customs
on Roman discipline in Books XXXVIII and XXXIX, and growing
arrogance towards foe and ally alike in XLII and XLIII.

It is possible to conclude that Livy himself saw a
double importance in his second pentad. Its dramatic
structure and style marked the advent of a new, maturer
phase in his writing. Dramatic form was enlisted for the
first time to give shape to the ongoing movement and
development of history. Equally important, however, was the
special significance of this period for Roman history. His
statement (IX.16.19) that this period was the wealthiest
in examples of good conduct probably does refer in the
first instance to the great individuals like Papirius
Cursor. Even more important, however, were the great
strides made by all Romans, whose moral learning we have
discussed at length. It was in these days that Rome entered
upon that Golden Age which he so idealized and so desperately
wished to recover in his own times. It is very possible
that, in Livy's mind, Books VI-X were the most important of
all the extant books.

---

[1]Earlier the speech of Cato on the spread of avarice
and luxury at XXXIV.2-4 handles moral issues at length.
His concern, however, is primarily for the future
(XXXIV.4.1-3); see Luce, Livy 252-253.

SELECT BIBLIOGRAPHY

Anderson, W. B. "Contributions to the Study of the Ninth Book of Livy," TAPhA 39 (1908) 89-103.

_____. Livy, Book IX. Cambridge 1909.

Badian, E. "The Early Historians." In Latin Historians, ed. T. A. Dorey. London 1966. 1-38.

Begbie, C. M. "The Epitome of Livy," CQ 17 (1967) 332-338.

Briscoe, J. "The First Decade." In Livy, ed. T. A. Dorey. London and Toronto 1971. 1-20.

_____. A Commentary on Livy. Books XXXI-XXXIII. Oxford 1973.

Broughton, T. R. S. The Magistrates of the Roman Republic. Vol. 1, New York 1951. Vol. 2, New York 1952. Supplement, New York 1960.

Burck, E. Die Erzählungskunst des T. Livius. Berlin 1934. Reprinted with a new introduction, Berlin/Zurich 1964. (Cited Burck, Erzählungskunst.)

_____. Einfürhung in die dritte Dekade des Livius. Heidelberg 1950.

_____. "Zum Rombild des Livius. Interpretationen zur zweiten Pentade." In Vom Menschenbild in der römischen Literatur, ed. E. Lefevre. Heidelberg 1966. 321-353.

_____. "The Third Decade." In Livy, ed. T. A. Dorey. London and Toronto 1971. 21-46.

Bruckmann, H. Die römischen Niederlagen im Geschichtswerk des T. Livius. Diss. Munster 1936.

Carney, T. F. "Formal Elements in Livy," PACA 2 (1959) 1-9.

Catin, L. En lisant Tite-Live. Paris 1944.

Cavallin, S. "Avant Zama. Tite Live XXX 29-31," Eranos 45 (1947) 25-36.

Columba, G. M. "L'Unificazione d'Italia nei Libri di Tito Livio." In Studi Liviani. Rome 1934. 135-158.

Dorey, T. A., ed. Latin Historians. London 1966.

Dorey, T. A., ed. Livy. London and Toronto 1971.

Dutoit, E. "Silences dans l'oeuvre de Tite-Live." In Mélanges J. Marouzeau. Paris 1948. 141-151.

Grant, M. The Ancient Historians. New York 1970.

Hands, A. R. "Sallust and Dissimulatio," JRS 49 (1959) 56-60.

_____. "Three Passages in Livy, I-V," Hermes 104 (1976) 250-251.

Heinze, R. Die augusteische Kultur. Leipzig and Berlin 1930.

Howard, A. A. "Valerius Antias and Livy," HSPh 17 (1906) 161-182.

Hunt, E. "Laudatores Temporis Acti," CJ 40 (1945) 221-233.

Jumeau, R. "Tite-Live et l'historiographie hellenistique," REA 38 (1936) 63-68.

_____. "Remarques sur la structure de l'exposé livien," Rev. Phil. 65 (1939) 21-43.

_____. "Tite-Live historien," Latomus 25 (1966) 555-563.

Kajanto, I. "Notes on Livy's Conception of History," Arctos 2 (1958) 55-63.

Laistner, M. L. W. The Greater Roman Historians. Berkeley 1947.

Liebeschuetz, W. "The Religious Position of Livy's History," JRS 57 (1967) 45-55.

Lind, L. R. "Concept, Action, and Character: the Reasons for Rome's Greatness," TAPhA 103 (1972) 235-283.

Lipovsky, J. P. "Livy." Forthcoming in Ancient Writers: Greece and Rome, ed. T. J. Luce. New York.

Luce, T. J. "The Dating of Livy's First Decade," TAPhA 96 (1965) 209-240.

_____. "Design and Structure in Livy: 5.32-55," TAPhA 102 (1971) 265-302.

_____. Livy, The Composition of his History. Princeton 1977. (Cited Luce, Livy.)

Madvig, J. Emendationes Livianae. Copenhagen 1860.

Martin, J. M. K. "Livy and Romance," G&R 11 (1942) 124-129.

McDonald, A. H. "The Style of Livy," JRS 47 (1957) 155-172.

_____. "The Roman Historians." In Fifty Years (and Twelve) of Classical Scholarship. New York 1968. 465-493.

Miller, N. P. "Tacitus' Narrative Technique," G&R 24 (1977) 13-22.

Momigliano, A. "Camillus and Concord," CQ 36 (1942) 111-120.

Murphy, P. R. "Themes of Caesar's Gallic War," CJ 72 (1977) 234-243.

Niccolini, G. "Le Lotte tra il Patriziato e la Plebe nell' Opera di Livio." In Studi Liviani. Rome 1934. 81-109.

Ogilvie, R. M. "Livy, Licinius Macer, and the Libri Lintei," JRS 48 (1958) 40-46.

_____. A Commentary on Livy, Books 1-5. Oxford 1965. (Cited Ogilvie, Comm.)

_____. "Notes on Livy IX," YC1S 23 (1973) 159-168.

Packard, D. W. A Concordance to Livy, 4 vols. Cambridge, Mass. 1968.

Ridley, R. T. "Was Scipio Africanus at Cannae?," Latomus 34 (1975) 161-165.

Robbins, M. A. S. Heroes and Men in Livy 1-10. Unpublished diss. Bryn Mawr 1968.

Salmon, E. T. "The Pax Caudina," JRS 19 (1929) 12-18.

_____. Samnium and the Samnites. Cambridge 1967.

Soltau, W. Livius' Geschichtswerk. Leipzig 1897.

Stadter, P. "The Structure of Livy's History," Historia 21 (1972) 287-307.

Suits, T. A. "The Structure of Livy's Thirty-Second Book," Philologus 118 (1974) 257-265.

Syme, R.   The Roman Revolution.   Oxford 1939.

_____.   "Livy and Augustus," HSPh 64 (1959) 27-87.

Ullman, B. L.   "History and Tragedy," TAPhA 73 (1942) 25-53.

von Fritz, K.   "The Reorganisation of the Roman Government
          in 366 B. C. and the so-called Licinio-Sextian
          Laws," Historia 1 (1950) 3-44.

Walbank, F. W.   "The Fourth and Fifth Decades."   In Livy,
          ed. T. A. Dorey.   London and Toronto 1971.   47-72.

Walsh, P. G.   "The Literary Techniques of Livy," RhM 97
          (1954) 97-114.

_____.   "Livy's Preface and the Distortion of History,"
          AJP 76 (1955) 369-383.

_____.   "The Negligent Historian: Howlers in Livy," G&R
          5 (1958) 83-88.

_____.   Livy and Stoicism," AJP 79 (1958) 355-75.

_____.   Livy, His Historical Aims and Methods.   Cambridge
          1961.   (Cited Walsh, Livy.)

_____.   "Livy and Augustus," PACA 4 (1961) 26-37.

_____.   "Livy."   In Latin Historians, ed. T. A. Dorey.
          London 1966.   115-142.

_____.   Livy, Greece and Rome.   New Surveys in the
          Classics.   No. 8.   Oxford 1974.

Weissenborn, W. and Müller, H. J.   T. Livi Ab Urbe Condita
          Libri.   Berlin 1860-1864.   (Cited Weissenborn.)

Wille, G.   Der Aufbau des Livianischen Geschichtswerks.
          Amsterdam 1973.

Witte, K.   "Über die Form der Darstellung in Livius'
          Geschichtswerk," RhM 65 (1910) 270-305, 359-419.

MONOGRAPHS
IN CLASSICAL STUDIES

An Arno Press Collection

Adler, Eve. **Catullan Self-Revelation.** 1981

Arnould, Dominique. **Guerre et Paix dans la Poesie Grecque.** 1981

Block, Elizabeth. **The Effects of Divine Manifestations on the Reader's Perspective in Vergil's** *Aeneid.* 1981

Bowie, Angus M. **The Poetic Dialect of Sappho and Alcaeus.** 1981

Brooks, Robert A. **Ennius and Roman Tragedy.** 1981.

Brumfield, Allaire Chandor. **The Attic Festivals of Demeter and Their Relation to the Agricultural Year.** 1981.

Carey, Chrstopher. **A Commentary on Five Odes of Pindar.** 1981

David, Ephraim. **Sparta Between Empire and Revolution (404-243 B.C.).** 1981

Davies, John K. **Wealth and the Power of Wealth in Classical Athens.** 1981

Doenges, Norman A. **The Letters of Themistokles.** 1981.

Figueira, Thomas J. **Aegina.** 1981.

Furley, William D. **Studies in the Use of Fire in Ancient Greek Religion.** 1981.

Ginsburg, Judith. **Tradition and Theme in the** *Annals* **of Tacitus.** 1981.

Hall, Jennifer. **Lucian's Satire.** 1981.

Hillyard, Brian P. **Plutarch:** *De Audiendo.* 1981

Hine, Harry M. **An Edition with Commentary of Seneca,** *Natural Questions,* **Book Two.** 1981

Horrocks, Geoffrey C. **Space and Time in Homer.** 1981

Lipovsky, James. **A Historiographical Study of Livy.** 1981

McCabe, Donald Francis. **The Prose-Rhythm of Demosthenes.** 1981

Parry, Adam Milman. *Logos* and *Ergon* in Thucydides. 1981

Patterson, Cynthia. **Pericles' Citizenship Law of 451-50 B.C.** 1981

Pernot, Laurent. **Les** *Discours Siciliens* **d'Aelius Aristide (Or. 5-6).** 1981

Philippides, Dia Mary L. **The Iambic Trimeter of Eruipedes.** 1981

Rash, James Nicholas. **Meter and Language in the Lyrics of the** *Suppliants* **of Aeschylus.** 1981

Skinner, Marilyn B. **Catullus'** *Passer.* 1981

Spofford, Edward W. **The Social Poetry of the Georgics.** 1981

Stone, Larua M. **Costume in Aristophanic Comedy.** 1981

Szegedy-Maszak, Andrew. **The** *Nomoi* **of Theophrastus.** 1981

Taylor, Michael W. **The Tyrant Slayers.** 1981

White, F.C. **Plato's Theory of Particulars.** 1981

Zetzel, James E.G. **Latin Textual Criticism in Antiquity.** 1981

Ziolkowski, John E. **Thucydides and the Tradition of Funeral Speeches at Athens.** 1981